D0862973

Charles W. Ore
An American Original

Irene Beethe, editor

Lutheran University Press
Minneapolis, Minnesota

Charles W. Ore
An American Original

Irene Beethe, editor

Published under the auspices of:
  Center for Church Music
  Concordia University Chicago
  River Forest, IL 60305-1402

ISBN: 978-1-942304-19-7

Lutheran University Press
PO Box 390759
Minneapolis, MN 55439
Manufactured in the United States of America

Contents

About the Center for Church Music

The Center for Church Music was established in 2010 on the campus of Concordia University Chicago. Its purpose is to provide ongoing research and educational resources in Lutheran church music, especially in the areas of congregational song and composition for the Church. It is intended to be of interest to pastors, musicians, and laity alike.

The Center maintains a continually expanding resource room that houses the Schalk American Lutheran Hymnal Collection, the manuscript collections of prominent Lutheran composers and hymn writers, and a broad array of reference works and resources in church music. To create a global awareness and facilitate online research, efforts are underway to digitize the hymnal collection, the manuscript archives, and the hymn festival recordings.

The Center publishes monographs and books covering various aspects of Lutheran church music.

The Center maintains a dynamic website whose features include devotions, presentations, oral histories, biographical essays, resource recommendations, and conversations on various topics in worship and church music.

The Center's Founders Group includes Linda and Robert Kempke, Nancy and Bill Raabe, Mary and Charles Sukup, and Waldemar B. Seefeldt, whose significant monetary gifts initiated the Center and have, along with the gifts of many others, sustained its momentum.

The Center's Advisory Board includes James Freese, Scott Hyslop, Linda Kempke, Jonathan Kohrs, Nancy Raabe, Carl Schalk, Steven Wente, and Paul Westermeyer.

Barry L. Bobb serves as the Center's volunteer director.

You can follow news about the Center on Facebook. Learn more about the Center and subscribe to its free e-newsletter at http://cuchicago.edu/about-concordia/center-for-church-music

Foreword

JOHN A. BEHNKE

Some creative people are totally absorbed in themselves and their work; and then there's Charles Ore, who is creative beyond belief, yet magnanimous with encouragement for others and care and concern for all. That's the Charles Ore I have experienced.

I found that out for myself years ago when my organ method book, *The Concordia Organ Method,* was published in 2000. I had taught organ in college for over 25 years at St. John's College in Winfield, KS, and at Concordia University in Mequon, WI, and during a sabbatical at Mequon I decided to put my thoughts together in one book. For me the book was an organizational exercise, just getting everything together in one spot so I could use it for teaching organ in the years to come. Besides, there were numerous organ method books by such stellar names as Harold Gleason, Catherine Crozier Gleason, Roger Davis, Richard Enright, George Ritchie and George Stauffer, and Flor Peeters that were beyond reproach. Over those first 25 years I had used portions of all these books. It was only on a whim that I sent this book to Concordia Publishing House for publication consideration. When they said yes to publishing it, I was pleasantly shocked and said that there needed to be one condition. It needed to be cheaper than the other organ method books, which cost $70. I hated telling students, trying organ for the first time, that they had to spend $40 on organ shoes and $70 on an organ methods book. They were expected to spend $110 and they didn't even know if they liked playing the organ. And then I thought to myself, some older, more experienced organ professors might well say that writing an organ methods book was a pretty gutsy thing for a "young" organ teacher to do, when there were all these other books by established teachers.

The first person to e-mail me after this book was published was none other than Charles Ore, who told me he thought it was a fine book. To say I was surprised was an understatement. Charles Ore was well known as a performer and a teacher, and the last thing he needed to do was reach out to me. This was the magnanimous Charles Ore that I have come to know. This is the magnanimous Charles Ore that many others have come to know, including Irene Beethe.

Some years later, Beethe, a graduate of Concordia in Seward, NE, began to study organ with me as she worked on her master of church music degree at Concordia University Wisconsin in Mequon. In our time together, she told me that during her days at Seward she had been the Ore's babysitter and that she knew the Ore family very well. She also loved the music of Charles Ore, like many of us. And when we talked about her recital and paper, I asked if she would like to write about and play music by her former teacher and "employer." To me it was a natural connection: she could write about someone she knew well, organize his compositions, and study his music in more depth. I was very glad as her teacher that she said yes and decided to take on this project. And so the research, the study, and the writing began.

I thought this project would not only be a worthy research project but also be good for the wider world of church music. Research is best when it contributes to the wider world. The teaching and publications of Charles Ore were known in Lutheran circles, but I thought and hoped that through this project Ore could be introduced to even more people in and outside Lutheran circles. And I thought Irene, with her study at Seward and her knowledge of the family, brought a unique perspective to this project.

Besides all these educational reasons, there is one other ulterior reason that I encouraged this research. It has to do with a wonderful small town in the state of Kansas: Winfield. It's a town that is an intersection for both Ore and me. Charles Ore grew up in Winfield, KS, where his family owned a farm. Winfield was also my home for eight short years from 1978 to 1986, when I taught at St. John's College and my wife taught at Trinity Lutheran Church.

Winfield is a small town where everyone knows everyone. We bought our first house there, which was a big deal to us. But for Winfield, it was never the Behnke house: it was always the Thompson house. The Thompsons owned the lumberyard for years and everyone knew where the Thompsons lived. Anytime you would call someone for anything, our address meant nothing. But all you had to say was that it was the old Thompson house and suddenly they knew exactly where you lived. This is the town that Ore and I both knew and loved. It was home to both of us. For me it was the Thompson house; for Charles I'm sure it was the Ore farm.

I'm thrilled to write this foreword for this very worthy Festschrift honoring Charles Ore, because I hope that Irene's wonderful work and the insightful comments of many others might very well introduce even more people in and outside Lutheran circles to the creative music of Charles Ore. His life and his music should be known to all church musicians. It's fine work, and I thank God for it and for Charles.

God's blessings on this important volume.

> John A. Behnke
> Professor of Music Emeritus
> Concordia University Wisconsin

Preface

In the summer of 1969, my sister was married. Her new brother-in-law worked in the registrar's office at Concordia Teachers' College in Seward, NE. Since I was going to be a sophomore in high school in the fall, he talked to me about the programs at Concordia. During these conversations he told me about the music department and an organ professor, Charles William Ore. Fast forward to the fall of 1972, and I am waiting in Weller Chapel at Concordia in Seward for my first college organ lesson with Ore. Little did I know that my initial encounter with the creative organ teacher would extend far beyond my four years as an undergraduate. Where did his imaginative spirit originate? What role did his family, education, and experiences play in his life, thus providing the realm of church music with compositions "on the progressive edge of contemporary classical church music"?[1]

In trying to answer those questions, I discovered that during Charles' formative years he was immersed in both Lutheran and Baptist hymnody. Perhaps this provided one reason for Barrett Spach's remark, "Charles plays with a Lutheran brain and a Baptist heart."[2] Charles' vibrant treatment of hymnody encourages congregational singing and enlivens the message of the text. His unique perspective on hymns is truly one of an "American original."

In celebration of his 80th birthday, it seemed "meet, right and salutary" to gather writers who, by their contributions, would enrich the lives of current and future church musicians and encourage them in their service to the Lord.

Notes

1   Ryan A. Winningham, "Cut from the Same Cloth? Two Perspectives on Music for Worship" (senior seminar in music, Hope College, 2003), 2.

2   Barrett Spach, quoted by Constance Ore, e-mail message to author, 16 April 2007.

Acknowledgements

This book is the culmination of a project begun nearly 15 years ago in graduate school. At first the efforts were directed toward a goal of achieving an advanced degree. However, as the correspondence with Charles and his wife, Connie, expanded into a deeper friendship, the project became more than an academic pursuit. In our conversations they graciously shared their personal and professional lives. I am deeply grateful for our visits, times that provided support and encouragement to a younger church musician.

I am thankful to John Behnke for suggesting I focus on Charles' life and music while I was at Concordia University in Mequon. The writers of the essays included here have, through their expertise, enriched the content of this volume. Two contributors to this Festschrift, Barry Bobb and Nancy Raabe, provided valuable editorial assistance throughout the entire process, enabling this publication to become a reality.

I am especially grateful to my husband, Ivan, for his constant support and encouragement throughout the life of this project.

Charles W. Ore: A Biography

IRENE BEETHE

Around 1700, the paternal ancestors of Charles W. Ore came to the Colonies. Without question the Ore family considered themselves to be *Americans*, fighting against the British in the Revolutionary War. Following the war victory and the gradual opening of the West, they moved from Virginia to eastern Tennessee. They continued on to Illinois, settling in Arenzville. Some of the family was involved in the Civil War. Since Charles' grandfather, John Calvin Ore, wasn't the oldest son, he sought further adventure by moving west to Kansas. In 1884, at the age of 21, John Calvin Ore settled in Cowley County near the community of Burden. John Raymond Ore, Charles' father, was born on the family farm in 1904.

Charles' maternal grandparents, John Williams (J. W.) Werling and Anna Barbara (née Fischer) Werling, were born in Allen County (New Haven), IN. Their parents had lived in the United States since the 1860s, immigrating from a German-speaking portion of Alsace-Lorraine (in present-day France). J. W. Werling was a graduate of Concordia Seminary in St. Louis, MO, and in 1922 he received a master's degree in German literature from Columbia University in New York City. Proud of their heritage, the Werlings spoke German at home in Winfield, KS, in the 1920s. A professor of German, J. W. Werling nevertheless felt that a side benefit of World War I was the acceleration of the process in which The Lutheran Church—Missouri Synod gave up German and moved to English, the common language of the New World. As a result, J. W. Werling's nine children learned English. Seven of them became teachers, nurses, or medical professionals.

J. W. Werling was a Lutheran minister, so when one of his daughters—Hilda Margaret—wanted to marry a Baptist—John Raymond Ore—the couple decided to elope, since the thought of a "mixed marriage" would have been difficult for their parents to accept. The parents of both the bride and groom were indeed quite shocked to hear the news of the marriage.

Charles William Ore was born on December 18, 1936, in Winfield, KS, to John Raymond and Hilda Margaret (née Werling) Ore and grew up on the same wheat farm as had John's father, 15 miles from Winfield. Charles' father had been raised Baptist and was *always* Baptist; thus Charles was at ease with Baptist hymns. Charles was raised as a Lutheran, however, and since hymns were an important part of his mother's life, she taught him Lutheran hymns. As a result, he was comfortable with hymns from both the Lutheran and Baptist traditions. When Charles was about five years old, his Werling grandfather sensed that Charles had musical talent. Consequently, his grandfather did what he could to teach Charles how to play piano: he taped the names of the notes to the piano keys and also penciled in the letters under the notes in the hymnal. This was how Charles learned to play Lutheran hymns.

One of the most important elements Charles enjoyed when growing up was the feeling that he was loved, especially by his parents and grandparents. He recalls many times "pounding on the piano"[1] as a young child would do, and his grandmother allowing him to do so, just because she loved him. Other neighborhood children wouldn't have been allowed such privilege. Given such freedom, Charles began to explore his musical personality at the most basic level. He "played" for hours. Since the piano in his home was in the living room, Charles was allowed to "focus on his music."[2] Many of the disruptions of today—television, computers, and stereos—weren't a part of his formative years.

Charles' mother, a teacher, had traveled extensively before meeting Charles' father and made the arts a priority in her life. When Charles exhibited musical talent, she sought out music education for him at an early age. His first professional piano teacher was Blanche Brookes in Burden, about five miles from home. She had studied with

Rafael Joseffy, the Hungarian-born pianist who gave up the concert platform for the life of a piano teacher. He cared little for fame or applause. Such an attitude certainly must have affected Charles' first teacher, for she was a legendary figure in the small town of Burden and was a superb teacher. Many times she could be seen with her old Studebaker full of her students traveling to concerts in nearby cities. Through her, Charles was encouraged to be imaginative in his music. Each week she would ask him, "Now, what's your piece for today?"[3] And he would present *his* music.

Charles' father was a farmer and had only an eighth-grade education, but he was supportive of music. He was always willing to drive Charles and sometimes his cousin, Janna Lee Ore, when it was necessary or recommended that they attend musical events in such Kansas communities as Winfield, Wichita, Hutchinson, Hays, Emporia, and even Lawrence, the latter a distance of about 150 miles.

Throughout Charles' youth his family still kept close contact with the Ore family in Illinois, including a great-uncle, Nelson Ore, the oldest of John Calvin Ore's sons, who was a fiddle player. The music that Nelson Ore played suggested an Appalachian folk-style influence. This diverse family environment provided a rich musical background for Charles, which is reflected in his compositional style.

While Charles was exploring the world of music through the piano, he also attended Old Salem School, part of the Kansas public school system, for the first seven years of his formal education. His mother and his grandmother taught there, and this is where his parents had met. This one-room school, about one mile from home, was more like a family. In his last year at Old Salem, the total enrollment was five students, one of whom was his first cousin. (For some of the years of Charles' attendance the school had had a few more students.) When Old Salem was closed for his eighth grade year, he attended a larger school, Cowley County School, a K–12 school in Burden. His class was ten times larger than his class of three at Old Salem School. He graduated from eighth grade in 1950.

During high school Charles continued his piano studies with Blanche Brookes; in all, he studied with her for 12 years, from 1942 to 1954. She valued creativity and continued to provide him with a wonderful atmosphere in which to develop his innovative spirit. Charles describes her as his "guiding light through his high school years."[4]

When Charles was 17 years old, Pauline Wenthe, the organist from his home church, Trinity Lutheran in Winfield, called him on a Wednesday to ask him to play the service for her on the upcoming Sunday. He had watched her play for 10 years and he accepted the challenge. Although Charles was quite proficient on the piano, playing many large compositions, his first instruction on playing the organ and service playing came that afternoon at the church. On the two-manual, tracker-action Kilgen with a straight pedal board, Mrs. Wenthe showed him the registration for the prelude, offertory, hymns, and postlude. She told him, "It'll be easy; there's nothing to it. Just use these stops, and play the bass notes [for the hymns] with the pedal."[5] Since he had no questions, she gave him the hymns and told him to practice. Charles recalls that this first endeavor at service playing went alright, although he is thankful it wasn't recorded! The parish pastor, Pastor Zehnder, rendered his support by singing along to help set the tempo. After this experience, Charles was hooked: he knew that organ playing, especially for worship services, was for him.

Charles graduated from Burden Public High School in 1954, after which he enrolled at the University of Kansas in Wichita to study medicine, though he still possessed a deep love of music. His advisor urged him to choose either music or medicine, since he couldn't pursue both. Choosing music, Charles then left the University of Kansas–Wichita and began attending St. John's Junior College in Winfield, where he received his first official organ instruction from Alma Nommenson, a graduate of Northwestern University in Evanston, IL. Charles remembers that, although he was a beginning organ student, she taught him her master's degree recital program: J. S. Bach's Prelude and Fugue in D Major (BWV 532), Charles-Marie Widor's Symphony No. 4, and Felix Mendelssohn's Sonata No. 1. Alma brought enthusiasm to her teaching and encouraged him in many ways. However, he had to teach himself about organ technique and had to figure out on his own how to play pedal scales on the organ. Charles graduated from St. John's in 1956.

Since St. John's was only a two-year college, Charles transferred to Concordia Teachers' College in Seward, NE. In this small Nebraska town he continued his organ studies with the fine organist and composer Theodore Beck. "Ted was a very caring teacher—he was demanding, but he provided lots of extra lesson time. He was one of the first to encourage me toward graduate school and university teaching."[6]

In 1958, at age 21, Charles graduated with a teaching degree and received his first call, to Trinity Lutheran School in Lincoln, NE, where he taught grades seven and eight and was organist and choir director. While in Lincoln, Charles approached Herbert Burton, the owner of Lincoln's fine arts station, KUCV, with an idea for an organ program featuring Nebraska organs, many of which had been built in the 1890s. Burton endorsed the proposal in order to spur interest in the history of music in Nebraska. Charles went on the road each week to a different church to record literature, usually in very cold spaces. (Did the sponsorship by a local mortuary have anything to do with that?) The recordings became the property of the radio station, and the station eventually became part of Nebraska Public Radio. "I'm sure that all of the recordings are lost—this is probably a very good thing!"[7] says Charles.

For two winters, 1958–59 and 1959–60, Charles studied with Myron Roberts at the University of Nebraska–Lincoln. "Myron introduced me [to] the many American composers and 20th-century French composers. I learned a number of Bach works with his direction. Most of his pedagogy was built on [Marcel] Dupré."[8] Charles remained in Lincoln until the spring of 1960.

On August 14, 1960, Charles married Constance Schau, whom he had met in a piano class at Concordia. Charles had already started graduate school part time (summers of 1959 and 1960) at Northwestern University (NU) in Evanston, IL. In fall 1960 the Ores moved to Evanston so Charles could attend NU as a full-time student. After Charles completed him master's degree in February 1961, he immediately began doctoral work at NU.

Theodore Beck, Charles' teacher at Seward, was Ore's connection into NU. Beck was also a doctoral student at NU and had already received his master's degree in music degree from NU and thus knew the NU music faculty well. He was able to introduce Charles to "many key individuals," including the chair of the NU music department, who was also the director of NU's symphony orchestra. "Because of Ted's recommendation, I became the organist of that organization. . . . That was just one of the many ways in which Ted helped to open doors."[9]

Barrett Spach was then the chair of the NU organ department. "Initially [when I began graduate studies] Barrett's schedule was filled so I studied with Tom Matthews. This was great for me, because Matthews was interested in improvisation." In the two years of study with Matthews (summers, 1959 and 1960), Charles was given many insights into the world of English organ playing. Ore had his organ lessons with Matthews at St. Luke's Episcopal Church in Evanston, where Matthews was also organist (until late summer 1960). "Matthews was a great player of 19th-century French music and was an outstanding service player. A wonderful teacher!"[10]

Charles was also privileged to study with Mildred Andrews for one summer while at Northwestern. She was quite a structured teacher and assisted him in improving his pedal and finger technique.

When Spach's schedule cleared a bit in fall 1960, Charles was able to study with him for the academic year 1960–1961. "Barrett knew the Chicago crowd, and [he] introduced me to [Jean] Langlais and [André} Marchal [both important players from France in the 60s]."[11]

While the Ores lived in Evanston they shared their home with a Moeller pipe organ that Charles had purchased from Trinity Lutheran Church in Grand Island, NE, in 1960. Five days of his Christmas vacation in 1960 were spent taking the organ apart and hauling the instrument home in the largest U-Haul he could find. The Ores' neighbors watched curiously as Charles moved the pipes, console, and other pieces upstairs to the spare bedroom in their apartment. Would the peace and quiet of their neighborhood be shattered? What they didn't realize was that Charles had no intention of playing this organ. He simply wanted to use it as a tool—to put the organ together and take it apart, over and over again, to see how the instrument worked. "Everything I know about organs I learned from the organ I took out of Grand Island."[12] However, Charles grew tired of moving it, and after several relocations and with children needing the bedrooms, the organ no longer had a place in their home. Isolated parts of the instrument can still be found, however. The organ fan frame decorated his office at Concordia. Some of the pieces are in storage, and a son-in-law organ builder inherited some parts.

In the fall of 1961, Charles began teaching at Concordia Teachers' College in River Forest, IL. One of his duties was to direct one of the choirs. David Jording recalls coming into a rehearsal while Ore was improvising on the piano. The choir members sat in amazement as they listened to him play "Silent Night" with a jazz beat. Another time, during a concert, the choir was looking "down in the face" because of some errors on the previous selection. Wanting to break the tension of the moment, Professor Ore "carefully pulled a water pistol from his inside pocket (seen only by us, of course) and pointed it at us. The tension broke, and we continued on just fine."[13]

Earlier in 1961, when Ore had been studying with Spach for only five months, the organist at Fourth Presbyterian Church in Chicago on North Michigan Avenue was relieved of his position. Spach recommended Charles for the position at this prestigious church, and Charles was brought in as their organist. However, his status at Concordia required that he relinquish the appointment after only five months. Shortly thereafter, one of the founding Lutheran Church—Missouri Synod congregations, First St. Paul in Chicago, was in need of a minister of music. The previous church musician, Theodore Beck's father, had died. Charles filled that post and served that congregation for five years, from 1961 to 1966. Once again, his relationship with Beck provided a wonderful opportunity for him.

When Barrett Spach died and Thomas Matthews left Northwestern, Ore then studied with Richard Enright, from 1962 to 1968. "He was a fine teacher—he knew a lot about organ pedagogy—he later wrote an organ method book. I worked on my first doctoral recital with Dr. Enright."[14]

Completion of Charles' doctoral work wasn't to happen at Northwestern, however. Many of his teachers at Northwestern either died or had taken other jobs. The organ department was experiencing much turbulence and eventually just fell apart. The completion of the degree was put on hold.

By 1966, Charles had taught at Concordia in River Forest for five years, along with such distinguished professors as Thomas Gieschen, Carl Schalk, Herbert Gotsch, and Richard Hillert. Feeling a need for increased freedom and expression and being a younger professor in an older music faculty, Charles accepted a position as assistant professor of music at Concordia Teachers' College in Seward, NE, his alma mater.

Concordia in Seward provided opportunities for Charles to work with his mentor, Theodore Beck. During his time in Seward he taught a variety of musicianship classes, worked with musical ensembles, and instructed hundreds of organ students. Charles also served with David Held, Art Fliege, Charles Krutz, Carlos Messerli, and more recently Kurt von Kampen, Jeffrey Blersch, and Joseph Herl.

As one of the organ professors at Concordia in Seward, Ore was able to put into practice his primary belief that teachers have a phenomenal influence, and that all teachers hold the key to unlocking the beauty of music to students. Charles feels blessed to have had so many wonderful teachers, each playing a different role in his training and striving to help him maximize his potential. As a professor, Ore had ample opportunities to put those ideas into practice, whether he was the cheerleader, disciplinarian, or encourager. So important to him were his students that he still has the notebooks from each year, recording what they played and how they progressed. To him, it was like keeping a diary of his children, to see how they've grown. (Of course, the books also contain his "secret code" for deciphering the notes!)

Many of his students have gone on to do graduate work, but graduate work wasn't necessary preparation for the goal he had in mind for each of them: to be church musicians. At Concordia, a "church college," the emphasis has always been on training students to work in congregations. Myron Roberts at the University of

Nebraska–Lincoln was also first and foremost a church musician. His influence is reflected in the manner in which Charles instructed his students, using hymns, liturgy, and chorale preludes as the core for the lessons. He is proud to say that the students at Concordia are 99 percent vocationally trained. Organists trained at a "non-church" university will focus more on different literature that is more geared for performance. Charles believes that the program Concordia offers is vital, since the organ is still used in churches today.

While continuing his teaching, Charles also became a doctoral student in 1982 at the University of Nebraska–Lincoln and studied organ with George Ritchie. Ritchie had the inside information about playing early organ music, having studied with Helmut Walcha and others in Europe. Charles felt Ritchie was on the cutting edge of performance practice related to seventeenth- and eighteenth-century organ literature. Ore's former teachers had taught more in the style of Dupré and others associated with the organ reform movement. "George changed the way I played and the way I taught. He updated my techniques."[15] Charles was finally awarded his doctor of musical arts degree in 1986.

Several times during his tenure at Concordia in Seward Ore was offered the position of chairman of the music division. Many times he refused because of the size of the job and the length of time before his retirement. However, in 1995 he was approached once more and this time said yes. He knew changes were on the horizon, and he was willing to spend his years before retirement improving the music department. As the head of the department he continued to look for changes for himself and for the future of Concordia's music program. "I believe there are three things to consider when looking into the future of music programs. They are curriculum, faculty, and budget, in that order. A large increase in technology will soon fill the musical world, and we will need specialized individuals to teach this to our students."[16]

Charles recognized that his predecessors had already realized the value of having a superior facility for Concordia music students: they had built the Music Center in 1966. So when in 1998 the school's name, Concordia Teachers' College, was changed to

Concordia University, Charles felt that now was the time to make the "good" department a "really good" department. In an e-mail message to President Walz, Charles presented the plan he had in mind. He wrote, "If we're going to be Concordia University, this is what it's going to take." Concordia needed to improve the curriculum and strengthen the undergraduate program. "A university can't just be [a university] in name only."[17] Walz helped Ore make it possible: he told him, "Do it!" The administration gave the green light to a major overhaul of the music department. The goal was accreditation from the National Association of Schools of Music (NASM), which would provide a stamp of approval for the institution's music department based on an external set of basic criteria for its programs.

NASM was founded in 1924 to promote better understanding among institutions of higher learning in the work of music. Through a national forum, the 610 institution members develop strength of purpose, maintain professional leadership, and establish minimum achievement standards for music. Accreditation of the Concordia music department by the NASM would grant music students graduating from this program recognition similar to that enjoyed by students in the accredited areas of law, accounting, and medicine.

Under Ore's leadership, the music department went to work to receive this endorsement from their peers in music education. During the next two years, following the initial evaluation in 1999, the music faculty rewrote the entire music curriculum, rebuilt the music library, and developed assessment tools. The department added a lab where students could compose using computer software and a synthesizer. As part of the process, faculty members sat on many committees and became masters at the art of compromise. Final approval came just a few months after Ore's retirement in 2002.

During all the adjustments, one principle has remained constant: Concordia's commitment to the Church, a service the music program has at its core. Congregations not necessarily associated with a school are looking for directors of music. Concordia's goal, and also Ore's philosophy, is to train young musicians into that role. Some of the situations that new graduates encounter require that they also assume the position of choir director. Good organists don't automatically make good choir directors, so a student training as an organist must also prepare to be a choir director. The requirements for a bachelor of parish music degree provide such instruction.

As Charles worked one-on-one with organ students, he educated them in music of such masters as Dietrich Buxtehude, César Franck, Olivier Messiaen, Vincent Lübeck, Mendelssohn, and Bach. However, as a teacher he was constantly on the lookout for new compositions to expand the student's musical repertoire. When he began to teach, the basic substance of hymnic material came from *The Lutheran Hymnal*.[18] With the introduction of *Lutheran Book of Worship, Lutheran Worship*, and several supplements,[19] however, the essential core of tunes had broadened. American hymnody and English hymns brought into the forefront new composers and melodies, adding tremendous breadth to organ literature.

In preparing students for their service in the church, Ore realized that "the make-up of the Concordia student body didn't represent the ethnic diversity of the typical American church." He felt that the "university must prepare students for this musical diversity while maintaining theological integrity."[20]

In his 35 years at Concordia in Seward, Charles encouraged students to develop their own musical lifeline, reflected by their compositions as well as those of others. Such teachers as Blanche Brooke and Thomas Matthews had fostered the spirit of improvisation in Ore, and this was passed on through him to his own students. Brooke created an environment for Ore that allowed him to explore his musical personality without concern about whether he was doing it "right." He provided his students with the same type of situation where they could create their own musical expression, in addition to helping the students develop good keyboard technique and learn the works of the masters.

True to his philosophy that he was training church musicians, Ore would equip them with the basic tools of improvisation usable in a worship setting—for instance, in hymn accompaniments, intonations, preludes, or postludes. In 1993 he revised an earlier paper that included quotations about improvisation and how its practice ebbed and flowed in the history of music. With this background, he provided guidelines to encourage his students to "try it" and to learn how two musical lines work together. Stressing to his pupils the need to begin with something they could control, Charles would have them start simply with a *note-against-note improvisation*—with the cantus firmus (a melodic theme) in the right hand and then with the cantus firmus in the left hand. The next step would be to use *two notes against each note of the cantus firmus* leading to *four notes against each note of the cantus firmus*. The improvisation might be in parallel, contrary, or oblique motion. Three of the basic building blocks of any composition are *repetition, variation,* and *contrast*. Charles would encourage his students to keep those ideas in mind, to assist both the listener and performer in "getting hold" of the piece. The final goals of improvisation were for the material to sound like it belonged together and for the students to enjoy the process of finding their own musical personalities.

Charles continues to hold seminars on improvisation and provides the participants with similar guidelines for improvisation and a list of what he likes to call "party tunes." In his opinion, these tunes enjoy letting you get hold of them and see how they are put together. One can "play" with such melodies as SLANE; JEFFERSON; DETROIT; IN DULCI JUBILO; FOUNDATION; ST. DENIO; LAND OF REST; VENI, EMMANUEL; ST. ANNE; ADESTE FIDELES; HERZLICH TUT MICH; WACHET AUF; GREENSLEEVES; WONDROUS LOVE; ENGELBERG; MADRID; STUTTGART; HOLY MANNA; LET US BREAK BREAD; and RESIGNATION. PICARDY seems to be the tune that "will go anywhere, in any way, in any key." The "least social" tune, in his estimation, is SINE NOMINE: "Once you start to take it apart, it sounds awful. That doesn't mean there aren't good pieces written on it. There just aren't many ways to deal with the tune—it is so tightly married to the text."[21] "It would be like trying to separate a couple married for 50 years!"[22]

Since improvisation has played a lifelong role in his musical development, Charles is not a believer that you can learn "how to" improvise in "15 minutes a day." Improvisation is a way of life and, like any other musical skill, it takes time to master. He has observed that children between the ages of four and seven *love* to improvise, exploring musical ideas freely, unencumbered by the critical ears of adults. Ore believes that when you improvise, you "make no mistakes," explaining that you can't correct it anyhow. He adds, however, that you may have some "internal bleeding," but you just need to go on.[23]

While Ore taught at the collegiate level at Concordia in Seward, he also held a "church job" at Pacific Hills Lutheran Church in Omaha, NE, to keep him in touch with what was happening in congregations. From 1975 to 2001 Charles was the cantor there, leading the choir and the congregation in the church's song as only he could, taking the common and making it extraordinary. During those 26 years he often wrote pieces for the musical forces that were at his disposal, catering to their abilities and limitations. Many of these organ compositions and hymn concertatos included virtuosic descants for trumpet or oboe for Kermit Peters and Grant Peters, father and son, who hold doctoral degrees in oboe and trumpet performance, respectively. The traditional choir verses were often written in unison for his 25-voice choir.

The connections between Concordia and Pacific Hills also benefited the new Catholic seminary south of Seward, St. Gregory the Great. A gentleman from Pacific Hills had an electronic organ he wished to donate to the music department at Concordia. Charles finally accepted the offer and for several years practice room 16 was the home of this instrument. Meanwhile, the seminary needed a practice instrument for their students. One evening, being informed that the room "just might be open," five students from St. Gregory came secretly and took the organ to the seminary. Students there used it for two years until the completion of their chapel. Ore played for the dedication of the chapel pipe organ in 2000. This amicable relationship fostered by Charles between Concordia and St. Gregory still benefits both institutions: students from St. Gregory attend classes at Concordia, and the chapel at St. Gregory provides a fine venue for concerts and recitals by the students from Concordia.

Following his official retirement from Concordia in Seward (2002) and continuing through the 2014–2015 academic year, Charles taught several organ improvisation and service-playing classes, invigorated by the students' enthusiasm and talents. While the years at Pacific Hills were enjoyable, he decided early in 2001 that he had driven to Omaha (a distance of some 70 miles) at 5:30 on

Sunday mornings long enough. In the fall of 2001, he was appointed to the position of associate organist at First-Plymouth Congregational Church in Lincoln, NE, a mere 20-minute drive from Seward. With the acceptance of this appointment, he had less time to compose because of the greater need for increased practice time. He enjoyed the Lied Organ [IV/110] built by Schoenstein. The variety of reed stops and five 32' ranks certainly offered a rich palette of sounds from which to choose. He said, "The job at Plymouth introduced me to hymn tunes that I would have never known—it has been an education in working with diverse materials."[24] In November 2006 Ore moved from associate organist at First-Plymouth to organist at First Presbyterian Church, also in Lincoln. This position provided him with more time for composition and provided another excellent venue for making music.

Charles' wife of 50 years, Constance, was both his most ardent supporter and a severe critic of his compositions. Her musical knowledge and understanding of his compositional ethos made her a valuable partner during the creative process. In January 2006 she was diagnosed with a rare blood disease, myelodysplastic syndrome. For nearly the next five years, Charles' compositional output lessened and, other than weekly service playing obligations and teaching, he set aside his professional life to care for his dearly loved wife. The disease consumed their lives as they grappled with the effects of different treatments and the hope that this invader in Connie's body wasn't as bad as reported. However, when all avenues for treatment were exhausted, they accepted the diagnosis as terminal. Their children and their children's families, who had long been a source of strength and joy for Charles and Connie, continued to bring joy and love for their parents with their frequent visits. In the last months of Connie's life they shared the responsibility of her care, including son John-Paul's relocation from the West Coast. His return to Seward provided Charles with another person to share the 24/7 care needed. Charles credits the support of their children as a priceless blessing, one that helped him continue living after Connie's death in 2010.

Charles began composing again in earnest about two years after her death. Even as he approaches his 80th birthday, he practices each day at Concordia, exercises to keep physically strong, and continues to explore new ways to use the full palette of the organ. He is careful to note that his collections are named *Compositions for Organ*, not chorale preludes. Always striving to learn, he has attended French organ music seminars in 2013 and 2015 and is preparing music to play at the 2017 seminar. By studying and performing European music on historic instruments, Charles has gained insight into the uniqueness of each organ and how it may have affected the compositions. One can only speculate how some of this knowledge will be incorporated into an upcoming Ore composition.

National radio broadcasts of *The Lutheran Hour* and *Pipe Dreams* regularly include music from Ore's four compact discs, each titled *From My Perspective*.[25] Charles estimates he has played between 200 and 250 organ recitals, dedications, and hymn festivals over the past 50 years. Hymn festivals offer a congregation a taste of Ore as a performer of the masters—he usually includes a large Bach work and a composition by another major composer—and Ore as an improviser of hymn tunes. Whether he takes the participants through the church year or focuses on one specific season, they are given the opportunity to experience hymns in a unique manner. The recent volumes of *Hymn Prelude Library*,[26] a collection of organ compositions on the hymn tunes in *Lutheran Service Book*,[27] contain several new compositions from this composer, who "desires to push the envelope"[28] and try things not done before, rather than duplicate what someone else has done.

Thanks be to God for his gift to the Church in the servant of Charles William Ore.

Notes

1   Charles W. Ore, interview with author, Seward, NE, 29 April 2005.

2   Ibid.

3   Ibid.

4   Charles W. Ore, quoted in Ryan A. Winningham, "Cut From the Same Cloth? Two Perspectives on Music for Worship" (senior seminar in music, Hope College, 2003), 1.

5   Ibid.

6   Charles W. Ore, e-mail message to author, 6 March 2006.

7   Ibid.

8   Ibid.

9   Charles W. Ore, e-mail message to author, 29 June 2016.

10 Charles W. Ore, e-mail message to author, 6 March 2006.

11 Ibid.

12 Charles W. Ore, quoted in "Music Tradition with a Vision: Striking a Chord," *Broadcaster* 78, no. 1 (Fall 2001): 4.

13 David Jording, e-mail message to author, 28 February 2006.

14 Charles W. Ore, e-mail message to author, 6 March 2006.

15 Ibid.

16 Charles W. Ore, quoted in Tracie Payne, "Charles Ore Unlocks Beauty of Music," *Broadcaster* 75, no. 3 (Spring 1999): 15.

17 "Music Tradition," 4.

18 *The Lutheran Hymnal*, authorized by the Synods Constituting the Evangelical Lutheran Synodical Conference of North America (St. Louis: Concordia, 1941).

19 Inter-Lutheran Commission on Worship, *Lutheran Book of Worship* (Minneapolis: Augsburg, and Philadelphia: Board of Publication, Lutheran Church in America, 1978); Commission on Worship of The Lutheran Church—Missouri Synod, *Lutheran Worship* (St. Louis: Concordia, 1982); *Worship Supplement*, authorized by the Commission on Worship, The Lutheran Church—Missouri Synod and Synod of Evangelical Lutheran Churches (St. Louis: Concordia, 1969); Commission on Worship of The Lutheran Church—Missouri Synod, *Hymnal Supplement 98* (St. Louis: Concordia, 1998).

20 Charles W. Ore, interview by author, Seward, NE, 3 August 2006.

21 Charles W. Ore, "Hymns for Improvisation" (presented at an AGO workshop, Kalamazoo, MI, 11 February 2006).

22 Charles W. Ore, "Hymns for Improvisation" (presented at an AGO workshop, Wauwatosa, WI, 22 October 2005).

23 Ore, "Hymns for Improvisation" (2006).

24 Charles W. Ore, e-mail message to author, 6 March 2006.

25 These CDs were originally published, 1992–2002, by Organ Works Corporation and are available from the corporation (2523 Bluff Road, Seward, NE, 68434). The discs are also available from Concordia Publishing House (1–3 only), Amazon, and CD Baby; or on Spotify and iTunes.

26 *Hymn Prelude Library*, ed. Kevin Hildebrand (St. Louis: Concordia, 2012-).

27 The Commission on Worship of The Lutheran Church—Missouri Synod, *Lutheran Service Book* (St. Louis: Concordia, 2006), 883, st. 3.

28 Winningham, 5.

Genuine American:
The Music of Charles W. Ore

NANCY M. RAABE

WILLIAM A. RAABE

In the American Upper Midwest, the slogan "Genuine American" often refers to the traditional values in which Midwestern culture is supposedly grounded.[1] But for the current purpose the term may be applied to the music of composer, organist, and teacher Charles W. Ore. For in its bracing originality, its boldness of vision, its diversity of approaches, and in the conviction that each piece has something important to say, Ore's music exemplifies much of what it means to be an American.

It is through these qualities of character, rather than by a classifiable compositional style, that one is able to identify Ore as the composer from the first few measures of a piece. In every encounter with the legacy of great hymns of the church, we find in his writing the deep devotionality of J. S. Bach, the energy of Hugo Distler, and the technical brilliance of Anthony Newman in his prime, as well as such strands of American popular culture as jazz and ragtime.

"While I am interested in all aspects of composition," Ore writes in the booklet accompanying each of the four CDs in his set *From My Perspective*, "it is primarily in the use of timbre, texture, and rhythm that I have tried to develop a style of writing that is indigenous to American culture yet reflective of historic traditions that have been used by composers for hundreds of years."[2]

As listeners, we must often hang onto our hats as Ore's creative imagination goes hurtling around each bend. But the music is hardly a free-for-all. In fact, each composition exhibits an admirable integration of motive, integrity of line, and clarity of form. At the final cadence (much as that might come as a surprise), we realize that the listening experience has been one of organic development. New life is being created in our midst by forces that have purpose and inevitability. We may witness a seed delicately planted that grows with symmetry and purpose into well-proportioned flower. Or we may experience seismic forces beneath our feet out of which majestic mountains, each with their own compelling design, come into being.

This combination of improvisation followed by carefully worked out structures forms the essence of Ore's teaching to his composition students. In a 90-minute video interview with former student Irene Beethe for the Center for Church Music's series Profiles in American Lutheran Church Music, he explains, "Students ask me, 'How do I get started?' I just say, 'Here's the pencil, here's the paper. If you have something to say, you'll find out how to say it. Write something down and we'll talk about it next week.'" Then when the next meeting comes, "Students bring me the paper and I'll say, 'It's not time to talk with you yet because you haven't thought about the idea.'" Ore is careful not to tell them what to write. Instead, he urges them, "You tell *me* what you want, and then we'll talk."[3]

Structurally Sound

Ore's introductions to his hymn-based compositions hardly sound like traditional preludes. They are so well formed that they could well stand on their own as the basis for an entire piece. Sometimes the propulsive opening ideas draw on the spirit, rather than the letter, of the hymn tune in question, so that it's a complete surprise when the tune enters. One case in point is "Let All Together Praise Our God."[4] The rollicking opening section is immediately engaging but bears no obvious relation to the hymn tune itself. So when LOBT GOTT, IHR CHRISTEN does swoop in, it is fully unexpected. Another example is "Jesus Has Come and Brings Pleasure."[5] Its first measure unleashes a torrent of sheer energy that swirls through the heavens, unchecked until JESUS IST KOMMEN, GRUND EWIGER FREUDE pushes its way into the maelstrom after 40 seconds, in Ore's own dynamic performance.[6]

The tune may also serve as the center of gravity through which a mighty wind churns, as in his "Festive Prelude on 'Come, Holy Ghost, God and Lord.'"[7] In the breathtaking coda, pitches are gradually piled upon themselves until it seems as if all the tones of the universe are colliding with each other in some kind of aural nuclear fusion. This energy finds release in the dramatic final cadence, which perfectly mimics the presence of the Holy Spirit that first Pentecost morning. Or, as in his beguiling "Earth and All Stars,"[8] the hymn tune may coalesce from fragments delicately placed in surprising spatial and tonal juxtapositions, as playful undulations (distant machines?) rumble beneath.

Ore's longer lines gain their shape and energy from sequential progressions that build impetuously and push the music toward the outer limits of expression. Who could have imagined the life-giving forces that erupt into the opening measure of his prelude on "A Mighty Fortress"[9]—as if Ore has tapped into some cosmic pipeline of sheer energy, perhaps from Martin Luther himself—and which carry through to the setting's cliffhanging final measures? And in terms of larger structure, "Let All Together Praise Our God" is a compelling example of a setting that brims with irresistible high spirits and jazzy rhythmic lunges, all of which are encased in a well-conceived and deliberately paced formal architecture.[10]

Concerning sheer creativity, only Charles Ore could have come up with the idea of couching ragtime and jazz within the context of the aural equivalent of film noir, as in his prelude for trumpet and organ on "Just A Closer Walk With Thee."[11] (See the beguiling performance on YouTube with Ore himself at the organ.[12]) And Ore's playful take on "I Am Jesus' Little Lamb" sports a winsome, dancing triple meter.[13]

Musical Influences

Improvisation figured prominently in Ore's musical formation from an early age. Ore notes that his very first piano teacher surreptitiously encouraged him in this endeavor. After each lesson, he recalled, "she would say, 'Now, Charles, before you leave, play me *your* piece.' I came to know that what she wanted was that she wanted me to improvise, to play something that was mine. So it was a routine that I had learned every week, to develop a piece."

Among Ore's strongest early influences were composers of the early- to mid-20th-century organ reform movement. "I absorbed music of [Hans Friedrich] Micheelsen and [Ernst] Pepping and [Hugo] Distler and [Siegfried] Reda and all the others associated with that new style," Ore says. "I became impressed with their rhythmic freedom, with their harmonic freedom, and how they could take elements and infuse those into church melodies, something that was just not being done [elsewhere]."

He notes that these influences are particularly audible in the ostinatos woven throughout his first set of *11 Compositions for Organ*.[14] "You'll find an awful lot of the organ reform movement from Europe, in little ostinato figures" in the manner of Pepping's *Kleines Orgelbuch* or in the music of Helmut Walcha. "I don't do that so much anymore; as life goes along, you become a different person."

However, Ore knew intuitively that this general style of organ music was not necessarily going to take hold in America. "Number one, we didn't have the acoustic spaces. And number two, we had collection-plate congregations—meaning that you couldn't just play 12-tone music and whether people liked it or not didn't make any difference. We were in a situation where we had a popular audience we needed to play for," meaning one that would need to lend its financial support.

Further, the nature of organs in the United States at the time, as compared to those in Europe, demanded other approaches. "Oftentimes the [American] instruments were not as . . . full of principals and mixtures and reeds on all divisions," he recalls. "We just didn't have a lot of access to those things at that time. But I came to realize that if I was going to write for the organ . . . I needed to have more interest in harmonies, in textures."

This need was fueled by his awareness that American halls didn't have the reverberation of those in Europe. "In the music of Franck, [Louis] Vierne, Widor, they have these three or four seconds of silence between phrases" because of the cavernous spaces, "in which there was sound going on. But here, when I took my hands up off the keyboard, it was gone."

Ore knew that if he was going to write for the organ, and if it was going to be used in America, he had to write in an entirely different style. "From the beginning I was interested in finding my way," using both classical and popular styles. The piano rag style of Scott Joplin exerted an especially strong influence on him. "I've got several pieces that reflect that. I think there were some people who were offended," Ore says with sly smile, "but so be it."

Characteristics of Ore's Music

A distinctive feature of Charles Ore's approach to writing music is that he calls his organ pieces compositions instead of preludes. "If people want to use them as preludes, that's fine," he says. But his deep motivation was to explore the organ as an instrument, using hymn tunes that connected him and his listeners to the church's history and to its rich musical traditions. "I wanted to be a part of that, but I wanted to find my way. I also felt I didn't want to write my next piece sounding just like the piece I'd written before. I wanted to find new ways, . . . new sounds."

If Ore's compositions sound as if they started out as improvisations, that's because they did. "No question about it," he says. Often he had no idea where the music came from. "Sometimes you're just sitting down and ideas come. If you don't write them down they tend to fly away and then they're gone." He eventually came to work with recording devices, transcribing the music from those improvisations. "They were germs of ideas that needed to be developed."

In terms of technical demands, these are not works for the faint of heart. Ore recalls that David Johnson (formerly of Concordia Publishing House) once asked him something to the effect of, "'Do you ever think about how difficult your pieces are when you write them?' I said to him, 'No.' I write them for myself. I tried not to make them any more difficult than they need to be in order to express what I feel."

* * *

The authors are blessed to have developed a working relationship with Charles over the years. Over the past two decades we have commissioned him to write several concertato settings of major hymns of the Lutheran tradition, including "O Morning Star, How Fair and Bright;" "O Day Full of Grace;" "Rise, Shine, You People;" "When in Our Music God Is Glorified," whose introduction is published in abridged form in set 7 of the *11 Compositions for Organ*; and most recently, "Christ Is Made the Sure Foundation." Some of these include preludes that have been published separately, such as that for "O Morning Star" in his *11 Compositions for Organ*, set 6. Ore plans the same for "Christ Is Made the Sure Foundation."

"O Morning Star, How Fair and Bright" (1993–94)

Charles once told us that his wife Connie (who died in 2010) considered "O Morning Star" to be his finest work. He also says he gets more requests for this piece on his tours than anything else he's written. It is a fitting tribute to Philipp Nicolai's hymn, which Lutherans have long heralded as the "Queen of Chorales."

Prelude (Manuscript)

The ravishing prelude to "O Morning Star" for trumpet and organ originally served as the introduction to the concertato. After the brilliant movement that serves as introduction in the published score took its place, the prelude was eventually published separately.[15]

Ore creates here a shimmering context in the manuals for the trumpet's warm intonation of the tune. Light glints and sparkles through alluring lines that wind themselves alluringly around the tune and between its phrases. But there is great compositional intent beneath this shining exterior. While each phrase of the tune in the trumpet is prepared with the greatest love and care, Ore's inventive use of harmony not only prevents the first-time listener from anticipating the appearance of each phrase but it leads us astray just when we think we're almost home. (See the example below, especially mm. 35–39.)

The setup for the arrival of the tune's final phrase is one of Ore's most winsome moves. In m. 35, at the end of the third phrase, poised precipitously on a fermata, the music begins to move slyly toward the area of the subdominant at a time in which we would customarily expect to be preparing for the final phrase in the tonic. In this connective tissue (mm. 36–39), Ore uses a motive in the upper register that *was* in the tonic earlier, so possibly only those with perfect pitch would be aware they're not where they think they are. The first note of the final phrase of the hymn tune therefore enters in m. 40 on the right pitch (D) but in the wrong harmonic region—that of the subdominant. As the music moves back toward the tonic and we become aware of where we've really been, our experience of the melting subdominant at that crucial point makes our experience of the music even more tender.

"O Morning Star, How Fair and Bright," Prelude, m. 33–40. Copyright © 1996 CPH. Used by permission. All rights reserved.

Introduction and Stanzas 1–6 (Published Score)

In the manner of Bach at his virtuosic best, the published introduction for trumpet and organ bursts forth like a racehorse from the gate and doesn't let up until the cadence 34 measures later. Typically for Ore, the primary thematic material bears no direct relation to the tune but instead sports its own personality. The trumpet takes on the hymn tune, straightforwardly at first but then with increasing flights of ornamental fancy. Near the end of the tune's third large phrase, this makes for a head-turning upward leap as the tune dances to its conclusion.

Stanza 1 includes the option for a well-shaped instrumental descant and the use of brass. Stanza 2, for women only, features an oboe part whose ardent yearning and eager, restless expectation draws out deeper meanings in the text ("Come, heav'nly bridegroom, light divine, / And deep within our hearts now shine; / There light a flame undying"). Most delightfully, at the last note of the penultimate phrase of text in m. 64 ("Now, though daily / Earth's deep sadness may perplex us / and distress us"), the tune itself settles on the lower tonic, D, while the oboe finds itself perched nonchalantly on a major seventh above (C-sharp). Stanza 3 offers another trumpet descant, and stanza 4 for men only has an optional oboe doubling the lithe counterpoint in the organ.

Stanza 5 plunges us back into the virtuosic spirit of the introduction but with the energy dialed up a notch. The trumpet (doubling the organ's right hand) unleashes a whirlwind of sixteenth- and thirty-second-note patterns that are actually an intensification of the music from the introduction. The effect is breathtaking, but it makes for a lip-splitting trumpet part! Between trumpet episodes, the chorale tune dances through the texture in the three lower voices with the sopranos providing a lively descant.

In the last phrase we encounter once again the startling upward leap mentioned above, but now the word on which it falls reveals its purpose to be intense longing for Christ's return: "Come, Lord Jesus! Crown of gladness! We are *yearning* / For the day of your returning."

A restatement of the opening material then begins, but after two measures the listener is startled to find the music wrenched upward a half-step from the key of D to E-flat. Ore is paving the way for stanza 6 in the new key, its higher position intensifying the music's affect. But what the modulation really means is that the nearly exhausted trumpeter must leap up to a concert E-flat instead of a D, two octaves and a third above middle C, at the movement's crowning moment! (See the example below.) Full forces then "break forth in sound," "gaily blending" to celebrate the King of Glory.

A word about tempo: Ore marks the Introduction "Brightly, ♪ = 100." Publisher websites where the piece is featured follow this instruction precisely. But Ore himself takes it at a much faster clip of ♪ = 126, and others are advised to do the same—stanza 5 included, if humanly possible. This keeps the music from becoming ponderous and allows it to unfold naturally.

In the afore-mentioned video interview, Ore reflects on this remarkable work:

> Once I decided to write on 'How Lovely Shines the Morning Star,' I was delighted to go and greet it. The text was there and the melody was there. But exactly what now do we do with it? Paul Bunjes [longtime professor at Concordia University Chicago in River Forest, IL] gave me these words: 'Think about hymn tunes as mannequins.' What you do is you put clothing on them and dress them in different ways. You have a lot of variety of clothing in your wardrobe; when you come back the next time, you assume they're going to have a different look. So I tried to imagine what kind of clothing 'How Lovely Shines the Morning Star' should wear. That's how I got started working on it.

Our invitation to Charles to create a concertato on this hymn is part of a commissioning program that we initiated a quarter-century ago. Typically we identify composers whose music we admire and ask them for a work for choir or instruments (or both) on a particular hymn tune. Often the tune is one that we feel is underserved by the body of sacred choral repertoire. This personal program has given birth to some 75 works by leading Lutheran composers of our day.[16] We have also commissioned hymn texts from Susan Cherwien, Gracia Grindal, and others. We ask the artists to name their fee; about the musical works themselves, we request only to specify the dedication line.[17]

For "Morning Star," the dedicatee was our son Martin. At the time, Martin was a toddler. But this bit of information was not included in the request for the work, which was conveyed to Charles by our friend Ann Siverling Kirchhoff, since we had not yet met him. Eventually Charles asked her, "Who is this Martin Raabe, anyway?" To his surprise, she replied, "He's a rambunctious two-year-old."

In his interview Ore kindly acknowledges our commissioning program and mentions this piece in particular. "The Raabe family has been extremely helpful in encouraging composers in the church and commissioning works. For example, there's 'How Lovely Shines the Morning Star.' At the time I didn't know who I was writing it for—and it turned out that I was writing it for their two- or three-year-old! I didn't know that!"

To us this is particularly delightful since, to our ears, the music of the introduction—and especially its impetuous twists and turns in stanza 5—mirrors Martin's cheerful rowdiness at that age, particularly in the thirty-second notes.

"O Morning Star" stands as perhaps Lutheranism's finest hymn. Ore's concertato confirms that standing and gives us the finest take on it that Americans have to their name.

"When in Our Music God Is Glorified" (1995)

Ore's concertato on ENGELBERG ("When in Our Music God Is Glorified") has an entirely different personality from "Morning Star," although the two were written within a few years of each other. Its distinctive character is rooted in the celebratory text and shaped by the heroic tune. As Paul Westermeyer describes the power of Charles Stanford's tune, its pulse "is so strong that the long notes at phrase ends never sit down but are always propelled onward with enough space for breath."[18] Its eleven measures unfurl in four phrases, each 3 + 3 + 3 + 2, with such propulsion that it stands as one of those rare tunes to end on the scale degree of the upper tonic. (Another that does this is Carl Schalk's THINE.)

Like much of Ore's music, the piece can be heard on CD, iTunes, and Spotify. But this concertato deserves to be made available in print to be used regularly by all Lutheran congregations, given the hymn's prominent use in worship and the insights its text brings to the congregation. It was nominated for the 1997 Pulitzer Prize in Music.

In his manuscript Ore offers the conductor seven performance options. Most involve choices concerning the two choral stanzas and the interludes between stanzas, some of which feature new material while others draw from elements in the Prelude/Introduction. The concertato remains unpublished except for a version of the opening movement that is shortened from the original by 11 measures. This appears in set 7 of the *11 Compositions for Organ.* Even so, there it occupies six full pages.

In the manuscript, the Prelude/Introduction stretches across 91 measures in dancing compound triple and duple time. Even with its strongly improvisatory impetus, closer scrutiny reveals a methodical structure uniting its seemingly disparate parts. Key elements are used as building blocks for the interludes to come. The entire movement is reproduced on the following pages.

A brassy fanfare without motivic definition immediately establishes great forward momentum and gallops across the first 12 measures. (Except for the first measure, this is the material omitted from the published version in set 7.) Emphasis on the flat seventh degree infuses the setting with an aura of timelessness, even at this early stage.

The *fortissimo* climax in m. 12 sets the stage for the movement's core thematic material in mm. 13–21. Propulsive in nature, rhythmic units combine to form a long, arching line of great strength and purpose, even with its unconventional construction. This extended idea arguably surpasses the hymn tune itself in power and virtuosity, appropriate for the subject matter of the hymn text.

Announced in the trumpets in m. 13 (the brass parts are doubled by the organ for much of the movement) and also emphasizing the flat seventh, this motivic material propels itself upward by means of sequence and extension. In m. 15 the motive ascends to the second degree, then to the fourth, then to the raised fifth, then to the sixth degree—harmonized by the submediant but here wrenching itself up to a surprising G-sharp—until it reaches the high point in m. 19 a ninth above where it began. The release of tension from this high point opens onto a bold statement of the first two phrases of the hymn tune by the lower brass, the first note of which overlaps with the last half-measure of the preceding section.

On the last note of the tune's second phrase we find ourselves surprised by a three-measure transition that leads to a restatement of the entire core thematic section. from m. 13 to m. 21. Out of this, the third phrase of ENGELBERG emerges confidently in the lower brass from m. 45 to m. 50.

But Ore has a bigger eye-opener up his sleeve: the last note in the phrase refuses to budge. As it is sustained through the next three measures, the organ launches into what seems at first to be a wild cadenza. A few measures later the brass enters with an arpeggiated counter-motive; this evens out into a dotted-quarter ostinato whose pitches prefigure the hymn tune's penultimate measure. At the same time, the organ "cadenza" intensifies into riveting patterns of contrary motion in the manuals.

In mm. 60–62 the brass sounds the final phrase of ENGELBERG. Is the movement coming to a close? The organ and brass move in this direction by means of massive parallel chords. But as we reach the last note of the tune, we realize the harmony is all wrong—a dominant minor seventh chord underscored by the pitch of the subdominant—and the organ darts forward with six more cadenza-like measures. In yet another twist, this leads us in mm. 68–76 into another statement of the movement's core thematic section.

Lest we imagine we are now on the verge of a final cadence, Ore has "just one more surprise." In m. 77 the first three measures of ENGLEBERG sound calmly, in common time and in the tempo of the hymn itself. But there are clues that more is in store: the last note of the third measure ascends to the higher octave rather than the lower, and this note is harmonized by an expectant subdominant ninth. A fermata prolongs the listener's anticipation that something is about to happen. And it does: suddenly we are plunged into an even more intense cadenza-like section featuring wild arpeggios in contrary motion, doubled by the brass. The intensity is heighted by repetition and pitch, until brass and organ join together in the last three measures for a clear and jubilant statement of the tune's fourth phrase, concluding triumphantly on the tonic.

ENGELBERG - PRELUDE / INTRODUCTION

To the Lutheran A Cappella Choir
of Milwaukee, as commissioned by
Dr. and Mrs. William A. Raabe

Tune/ENGELBERG by Charles V. Stanford 1825-1924
setting © Charles W. Ore b. 1936

Stanzas 2 and 4

Ore offers a number of options in stanzas 2 and 4 of the concertato. Like stanza 1, stanza 2 may be sung by the choir and congregation with a trumpet descant. Alternately, the conductor may choose to use the choral version of stanza 2. Not to mince words, but the bizarreness of this stanza is outdone only by that of the choral option for stanza 4. Of course, both visions are born out of the hymn texts and proclaim their truth in new and arresting ways. However, their treatments suit their respective texts perfectly and truly bring to them a "new dimension in the world of sound." The first pages of each of these movements follow below.

Stanza 2 features the three lower choral parts and muted brass in a syncopated, tightly wound ostinato that extends through the entire movement save its last three measures. From a unison the ostinato slowly opens harmonically by means of modal descent all the way down to the lower tonic, with parallel-fifth undulations on the lower voices cloaking the text in an aura of mystery. Above this, the sopranos intone a modal variation of ENGELBERG: "How oft, in making music, we have found / a new dimension in the world of sound."

At the third phrase, "as worship moved us to a more profound," the upper voices in the ostinato widen into tritones; over the continuing parallel fifths in the lower voices, the harmonies take on a wandering dominant-seventh character with no tonal direction. This continues with increasing urgency and spills over into the first of many repeated Alleluias. These rise higher and higher in tessitura, reaching up to an almost-impossibly high A-sharp in the sopranos.

Repetition of this climactic two-measure phrase heightens the suspense and makes the return to the lower octave more dramatic than it would have been otherwise. Here the entire stanza of text is reiterated and moves into the final Alleluia by means of a cadence featuring an augmented sixth in second inversion. This resolves to a first-inversion tonic instead of directly to the dominant as one might normally expect, after which Ore concedes with a quick V-I cadence. By the way, the augmented sixth at that spot retroactively accounts for all those seemingly lost dominant seventh chords earlier, which have now have acquired meaning and purpose.

Like stanzas 1 and 2, the third and fourth can be sung simply with congregation. But Ore's stanza 4, couched in minor mode, transports us to a different world. The landscape is bleak and almost lifeless, constructed entirely of static two-measure ostinatos that are piled one upon the other.

First to enter is a plucked double bass, which mutters dispiritedly up the scale and back down. Then the organ joins with a syncopated pattern of descending parallel minor-mode triads, with the added second for a subtle jazzy effect. Together with the double bass this paints a distant, ominous picture. But where are we? What is this place of foreboding to which Ore has transported us?

The choir women then enter with a form of the minor-mode variant of ENGELBERG we encountered in stanza 2. They sing, "And did not Jesus sing a song that night / when utmost evil strove against the light?" Now we see: we are with Jesus and the disciples in the Upper Room after that last Passover meal as they sing their hymn (Mark 14:26, Matthew 26:30). At the same time, we can also see the unfolding of the Passion narrative from the Mount of Olives to Gethsemane and finally to Golgotha.

As the text reaches the Alleluia, the women's part dissipates into another two-measure ostinato, this one moving in parallel fifths. Another, more restless in character, enters in the oboe. This makes for a fascinating quartet of interlocking ostinatos of varying tones, timbres, and rhythms. These relentless ostinatos suggest a sense of despair: for Jesus' life on earth in mortal form, "it is finished."

Not long after, the upper three parts begin to fade away as mysteriously as they arrived. The oboe and women are first to go, followed by the organ. The lonely double bass finally comes to rest on the lower tonic. This finality, perhaps, incites the oboe to mournfully intone the last phrase of the tune in minor mode. The double bass plucks a series of static quarter notes that seem to spell the end of hope. There are few text-paintings in the canon as moving as this one.

But there is new life: at precisely this point, the organ's right hand returns very softly with the chord cluster from its ostinato, but now with a *major* third. This hovers expectantly in midair until suddenly the music from the second (even wilder) organ cadenza in the Prelude/ Introduction erupts onto the scene. Thundering parallel fifths in the pedals announce the arrival on the tonic. This leads directly to stanza 5, featuring congregation, descant, and festive brass parts.

In the manuscript, Ore includes options for interludes between stanzas. After the choral version of stanza 2, a fanfare-like passage in common meter emphasizes the flat sixth and seventh scale degrees and is rife in parallel fourths and fifths.

Ore specifies a more extensive interlude following the choral option for stanza 4. Here we find building blocks from the Prelude/Introduction appropriated and rearranged. It starts off with the non-motivic fanfare from the beginning, which leads (as before) into the main motivic material. Into this, however, Ore inserts "all choirs" that sing the text of the hymn's first stanza *to the music of this main section.* In its relentless, determined ascent, it's every bit as challenging for the voices as for the high trumpets. And what happens on the last word of text? We are plunged back into the second of the Prelude/Introduction's contrary-motion cadenzas, with brass blaring. This leads, as before, to a full cadence. How fitting a setup it is for the hymn's final stanza, with the congregation and all forces announcing, "Let ev'ry instrument be tuned for praise"!

Postlude

The Church benefits greatly from Charles W. Ore's insights and creativity. Every Lutheran organist must master at least one of Ore's compositions to fully appreciate the gifts that Ore brings to bear and to share those gifts with worshippers in context.

Charles Ore's contributions to the church are diverse, insightful, and uniquely American. His creative imagination moves us from two dimensions on a page into that multidimensional world in which the combination of text and music gives birth to a new order, one that will endure for eternity.

Engelberg v. 2 CHOIR

Engelberg v. 4 CHOIR

To the Lutheran A Cappella Choir
of Milwaukee, as commissioned by
Dr. and Mrs. William A. Raabe

Text : F. Pratt Green

Music © Charles W. Ore

Notes

1. Judith T. Kenny and Jeffrey Zimmerman, "Constructing the 'Genuine American City': Neo-Traditionalism, New Urbanism and Neo-Liberalism in the Remaking of Downtown Milwaukee," *Cultural Geographies* 11, no. 1 (January 2004): 74–98, http://cgj.sagepub.com/content/11/1/74. The slogan was in official use from 1995 to 2005.

2. These CDs were originally published, 1992–2002, by Organ Works Corporation and are available from the corporation (2523 Bluff Road, Seward, NE, 68434). The discs are also available from Concordia Publishing House (1–3 only), Amazon, and CD Baby; or on Spotify and iTunes. The quote is from Charles W. Ore, accompanying booklet, *From My Perspective 2*, Organ Works Corporation CD (1995).

3. Charles W. Ore, interview by Irene Beethe, Seward, NE, April 2015, https://www.cuchicago.edu/about-concordia/center-for-church-music/profiles-in-american-lutheran-church-music/video-interviews/; click on "Charles Ore." Unless otherwise noted, all quotations by Ore are taken from this interview.

4. Charles W. Ore, *11 Compositions for Organ*, set 6 (St. Louis: Concordia, 1995).

5. Charles W. Ore, *11 Compositions for Organ*, set 5 (St. Louis: Concordia, 1991).

6. Charles W. Ore, *From My Perspective*, Organ Works Corporation CD (1992).

7. Charles W. Ore, *11 Compositions for Organ*, set 9 (St. Louis: Concordia, 2012).

8. Charles W. Ore, *11 Compositions for Organ*, set 4 (St. Louis: Concordia, 1989).

9. Charles W. Ore, *11 Compositions for Organ*, set 8 (St. Louis: Concordia, 2008).

10. Ore, *11 Compositions for Organ*, set 6.

11. Charles W. Ore, *Three for Two: Spiritual Expressions for Keyboard and Instrument* (St. Louis: Concordia, 2013).

12. Recorded 2 March 2014 at First Presbyterian Church, Lincoln, NE, https://www.youtube.com/watch?v=v2GdZOrolms.

13. Ore, *11 Compositions for Organ*, set 5.

14. Charles W. Ore, *11 Compositions for Organ*, set 1 (St. Louis: Concordia, 1971).

15. It appears in Ore's *11 Compositions for Organ*, set 9.

16. A full listing of commissions may be found at http://nancyraabe.com/images/commissions.pdf.

17. William Raabe discusses the commissioning program in an interview with Steven Wente, River Forest, IL, June 2015, https://www.cuchicago.edu/

about-concordia/center-for-church-music/profiles-in-american-luther-an-church-music/video-interviews/; click on "William Raabe."

18   Paul Westermeyer, *Hymnal Companion to Evangelical Lutheran Worship* (Minneapolis: Augsburg Fortress, 2010), 275.

The Choral Compositions
of Charles Ore

DAVID HELD

Charles Ore is best known for his organ compositions. His nine volumes of *11 Compositions for Organ*, which appeared from 1971 to 2012, comprise the longest-running series in Concordia Publishing House history. (A tenth volume will be published in 2017.) However, he also has written many choral compositions that were published by Augsburg Publishing House (1976–83), by Concordia Publishing House (1981–98), and by MorningStar Music Publishers (1991–98).[1] A complete listing of his choral compositions may be found in Appendixes A, B, and C following this essay. These appendixes are based on the listing in Irene Beethe's master's thesis, "Charles W. Ore: From 'My' Perspective."[2] (She assigned all the compositions an OWC number. This number is not related to Organ Works Corporation, but is merely a numbering system. These numbers are used throughout this essay.)

Concerning his music, both organ and choral, Charles writes, "While I am interested in all aspects of composition, it is primarily in the use of timbre, texture, and rhythm that I have tried to develop a style of writing that is indigenous to American culture yet reflective of historic traditions that have been used by composers for hundreds of years." Also, as may be seen in many of his choral works, he is very much in favor of congregational involvement: "This active participatory style of congregation singing is both a treasure to be preserved and a fragile cultural phenomena that is always in danger of being lost or set aside."[3]

Lutheran Book of Worship appeared in 1978 and *Lutheran Worship* in 1982.[4] Both of these volumes placed a renewed emphasis on the singing of psalms. They also each had a listing of hymns that were designated the Hymn of the Day. During the late '50s and through the '60s and '70s, hymn concertatos started appearing: Paul Bunjes' series began with his setting of "A Mighty Fortress Is Our God" in 1957.[5] The two hymnals provided an impetus for the composition of psalm and hymn settings that involved congregation, choir, organ, and instrumentalists.

In addition to Charles' responsibilities as organ instructor and university organist at Concordia Teacher's College (renamed Concordia University in 1998) in Seward, NE (1966–2002), he also served as cantor at Pacific Hills Lutheran Church in Omaha, NE (1975–2001). At Pacific Hills he worked with a fine choir, had a splendid Schantz organ, fine acoustics, and access to some outstanding instrumentalists. This church followed a liturgical pattern of worship, thus also providing a need for psalm and hymn settings.

I came to Concordia in Seward in 1979. One of my joyful responsibilities was directing the Concordia Singers, an auditioned choir of about 30 singers. The Singers began as a small liturgical choir within the Concordia A Cappella choir led by Paul Rosel in the 1950s. The Singers, expanded as an independent group during the 1960s and 1970s by Dr. Carlos Messerli, continued to function within the context of liturgical worship. Here, too, there was a need for psalm and hymn settings. The choir also usually sang for the festival services of the university—e.g., the Reformation service—in addition to singing at St. John Lutheran Church in Seward about once a month. This congregation, too, observed the practice of a liturgical service.

Since Charles was the university organist, we quickly found ourselves working together with the university chaplain planning the university festival services. At that time I knew Charles chiefly through his organ compositions. I remember thinking how great it would be if he would write some music for the Singers, but I was hesitant to ask him. We had had two years together as students during our college years, although since he was two years my senior,

I didn't get to know him too well. Thus I was most pleased when in the middle of my first year leading the Singers he told me I should feel free to ask him to compose a piece for the Singers.

That summer (1980) I approached him and suggested that he might write a psalm setting for us to take on tour. In January 1981 he wrote a setting of Psalm 31 (OWC 82) for us. It consisted of an antiphon for the congregation, a choral setting of the psalm text, and a solo line. The composition was very well received by the attendees at the concerts. That was the beginning of a long, warm relationship with him for the next 20 years. Psalm settings continued to be part of his compositional repertoire: over the years he wrote seven additional psalm settings. As will be seen later, he also wrote "Brother James Air/The Ash Grove" (OWC 103), which included a paraphrase of Psalm 23, and "The Lord Has Done Great Things for Me (OWC 212), which was based on Psalm 126:3.[6]

The next summer (1981) I asked him if he would like to do another composition. He was most receptive to the idea. Since the Singers toured over Holy Week and Easter, I asked him if he could write a Passion setting, but emphasized that he did not have to use the traditional Passion text. I also stated that maybe about eight minutes would be a fine length. As was his custom, he asked me what forces beside the choir were available. That year I had some excellent brass players and a number of soloists. During the first semester, Charles and his wife Connie worked on developing the texts to be used. They came up with a five-part text. During the J-term of 1982, he worked at the composition. When it was finished he came to me and told me to sit down, for the length of the work turned out to be twenty-two minutes instead of eight. During the course of the semester the Singers and I experienced the joy of having the composer join us in rehearsal to make some suggestions. That proved to be a procedure we often used in ensuing years. As things went along in rehearsing the Passion composition, neither he nor I were happy with the ending. So he reworked it to the satisfaction of both of us. "Father, the Time Has Come" (OWC 100) was written for SATB choir, three soloists, four-part brass, organ and congregation.

Hymn settings occupy much of Charles' choral repertoire. In 1983 he wrote a setting of "At the Lamb's High Feast We Sing"

(OWC 102).[7] It was scored for instruments (two clarinets, four-part brass choir), SATB choir, organ, and congregation. The introduction begins with the clarinets introducing a dance-like melody that is countered by the cantus firmus of the hymn played by a trombone. Eventually four-part brass and organ join in this introduction.[8] The disposition of the eight stanzas is as follows:

- st. 1—Congregation accompanied by a basically four-part organ setting;
- st. 2—Women of congregation accompanied by a free organ setting;
- st. 3—Men of congregation accompanied by an organ setting as in stanza 1;
- st. 4—SATB choir accompanied by a second free organ setting;
- st. 5—Congregation accompanied by an organ setting as in stanza 2;
- st. 6—SATB choir in a free style accompanied by an organ setting of the cantus firmus;
- st. 7—Congregation with trumpet descant and an organ setting as in stanza 2; and
- st. 8—Congregation with four-part brass descant and choir soprano descant.

This pattern of using congregation, choir, and varied organ accompaniments and instrumental combinations was followed in most of Charles Ore's hymn concertato settings.[9] On tour, congregations reacted quite positively when the Ore hymn settings were used. Often heard was the comment, "I've never realized that hymns could sound like this." At a series of Easter morning services on tour, we sang "At the Lamb's High Feast" in a 6:30 a.m. service. The pastor was so thrilled with the setting that at later services that morning, even though the hymn was not scheduled to be sung, he added the hymn to his sermon.

While on tour, the Singers invited local congregational choirs to sing with us. One of the pieces I chose in which to involve them was "Brother James' Air/The Ash Grove" (OWC 103).[10] This paired a paraphrase of Psalm 23, "The Lord's My Shepherd, I'll Not Want," using the melody BROTHER JAMES' AIR, with the hymn text "Let All Things Now Living," using the melody THE ASH GROVE. The disposition of the work is as follows:

> st. 1—BROTHER JAMES' AIR: SB choir in a canonic setting;
>
> st. 2—BROTHER JAMES' AIR: Congregation with a descanting instrument;
>
> st. 3—BROTHER JAMES' AIR: Choir trebles with a descanting instrument;
>
> st. 4—BROTHER JAMES' AIR: Choir or congregation with a descanting instrument;
>
> st. 5—BROTHER JAMES' AIR: Choir treble voices with a descanting instrument;
>
> st. 1—THE ASH GROVE: Choir male voices with a descanting instrument; and
>
> st. 2—THE ASH GROVE: Congregation with vocal and instrumental descant.

The local congregational choir was easily able to handle the vocal parts. The congregation enjoyed its participation in the variety of settings.

Connie Ore, Charles Ore's wife, served as music director of St. John Lutheran Church and its school. During the early 1980s the school prepared some outstanding Christmas Eve services. Charles wrote processional hymn settings for two of these services: "Oh, Come, All Ye Faithful" (OWC 79) and "Now Sing We, Now Rejoice" (OWC 101). A closer look at "Oh, Come, All Ye Faithful" follows. In addition to the hymn text and tune, a countermelody to the hymn was written using an independent text, which is used throughout the setting. This text, which is an amplification on the text of "O Come, All, Ye Faithful," follows:

> Come to our reunion, come Joseph and Mary,
> Come to our reunion, come shepherds, come all.
> Oh, reunite with our God, our God and Father.
> Come home through your Brother, the Christ child so small,

Come and behold him, born the King of angels,
Come to our reunion, come mothers and fathers.
Come to our reunion, come children, come all,
Oh, reunite with your God, your God and Father,
Come home through your Brother, the best Gift of all.

The setting begins with an organ prelude that introduces the "Come to Our Reunion" tune.

The hymn is then organized as follows:

st. 1—All children's choirs and available treble instruments sing "Oh, Come, All Ye Faithful." Later in the stanza the "Come to Our Reunion" text and tune is added to the cantus firmus.

st. 2—Congregation and children's choirs sing stanza 2 of the carol. The organ accompaniment is a standard hymnal accompaniment. Instruments and a few voices sing a descant to the carol. Following stanza 2 the choirs move to a slightly modified setting of the "Come to Our Reunion" text.

st. 3—Congregation sings stanza 3 of the carol. The organ has a free accompaniment. The choirs sing the "Come to Our Reunion" text and tune. Percussion instruments are an additional possibility. This is followed by the choir trebles singing a free text and two-part setting of a new melody and text, "Scattered by Sin."

st. 4—Congregation and choirs sing stanza 4 of the carol. Adult sopranos and tenors sing a descant. Both vocal parts may be reinforced with instruments. A handbell part utilizing two octaves is also available.

A similar approach is used in "Now Sing We Now Rejoice," which also utilizes a countermelody and implementation of varied vocal and instrumental forces.[11]

At both Concordia and Pacific Hills, Charles had access to fine instrumentalists. Two members at Pacific Hills were Kermit Peters, oboe professor at the University of Nebraska, Omaha, and his son, Grant Peters, who earned a doctorate in trumpet at North Texas State (now the University of North Texas). Many fine instrumentalists were also available at Concordia.

Thus a challenging trumpet part may be used in Charles' setting of "Our God, Our Help in Ages Past" (OWC 156).[12] It is scored for SATB choir, congregation, descanting instrument, and keyboard. The setting begins with an energetic organ and trumpet introduction. The hymn is then apportioned as follows:

st. 1—Congregation sings the hymn melody accompanied by a free organ setting and a choral descant.

st. 2—All men, both congregation and choir, sing the hymn melody with a free organ accompaniment.

st. 3—After a short transition, the choir sings a four-part choral setting with an instrumental descant.

st. 4—All women, both congregation and choir, sing the hymn melody with a new free organ accompaniment.

st. 5—Entering at staggered intervals, the choir sings the melody of the hymn. The accompaniment, based upon material used in the hymn introduction, may be by organ alone, but the addition of the instrumental descant adds energy to the setting. A modulation from C major to D major concludes the setting.

st. 6—Congregation sings the melody of the hymn accompanied by a vocal descant and an instrumental descant.

One of the hymn settings that involves oboe is "O Morning Star, How Fair and Bright" (OWC 173),[13] scored for SATB choir, congregation, solo trumpet, optional oboe, brass quartet (2 trumpets, 2 trombones), and organ. The introduction involves organ—using a theme that will be heard later in the setting—and trumpet—playing a melody based on the cantus firmus.

The treatment for each of the stanzas follows:

st. 1—Congregation sings the cantus firmus, sopranos sing and optional oboe plays a descant, and organ and brass quartet sound a varied accompaniment.

st. 2—Congregation and choir women sing the cantus firmus, organ plays a free accompaniment and descant, which may be joined by an optional oboe.

st. 3—Congregation sings in unison or in SATB, with organ and brass quartet.

st. 4—Congregation and choir men sing the cantus firmus, with the organ sounding a free accompaniment and with optional oboe on descant.

st. 5—Choir altos, tenors, and basses sing a melody based on material used in the introduction, sopranos sing a descant, and solo trumpet and optional oboe play material used in the introduction. Organ and trumpet/oboe modulate from D major to E-flat major.

st. 6—Congregation plus altos and tenors sing the cantus firmus, choir sopranos and tenors plus solo trumpet sound a descant, and organ and brass quartet have a free accompaniment.

The result is a brilliant sound that builds from the introduction to the final stanza. Not only the cantus firmus but also the accompaniments unify the composition. This type of procedure is often used by Charles in his hymn concertatos.

In addition to psalm and hymn settings, Charles has written compositions that use free texts.[14] Earlier reference was made to "Father, the Time Has Come." This would relate well to Holy Week, especially Good Friday. Additional examples of this type of composition are:

"A Time and a Purpose" (OWC 180):[15] scored for SATB choir, optional congregation, and keyboard. The text is based on Ecclesiastes 3:1–8 and Romans 8:28.

"This Is My Son" (OWC 176):[16] scored for SATB choir, optional congregation, trumpet, and organ. The choir text is taken from selected verses of Matthew 3. Toward the conclusion of the composition the congregation joins the choir in singing stanza 3 of the chorale "To Jordan Came the Christ, Our Lord." The organ accompaniment and choral parts are very rhythmic and contain an abundance of syncopation. The composition would be appropriate to use on Advent 3.

"My Crown of Creation" (OWC 127)[17]: scored for SATB and organ. The composition uses the text "My Crown of Creation" by Jaroslav Vajda and incorporates an adaptation of the Shaker tune "Simple Gifts." The stanzas tell the purpose of Christ coming to save us and also contain a remembrance of his life. At the conclusion of each stanza, the choir sings:

> Take heart, the best is yet to be! If you can see what
>   you mean to me,
> You will know the truth, and it will make you free,
> Once you see, my child, what you mean to me.

A rhythmic accompaniment is an integral characteristic of the composition. While most of the piece is in G major, an appropriate change to G minor is used for the stanza that speaks of Jesus being in the tomb. The final triumphant stanza returns to G major, with the final chorus moving to A-flat major. The final refrain is modified to include the words:

> Take heart, the best is yet to be! If you can see what
>   you mean to me,
> You can be the child I wanted you to be,
> My crown of creation, you are dear to me!

The result is an affirmation of the love and care shown to us by God, evident not only in the total text of the composition but also in the triumphant sound of the music.

Hymn settings were an important segment of Charles Ore's choral writing: he wrote 17 such compositions. The Concordia Singers were privileged to sing many of these hymn concertatos. I conclude this essay by referring to one of my favorite hymn settings, which was the last work the Concordia Singers and I did with Charles Ore, as well as the final composition I did with the Singers at the conclusion of the 2000 baccalaureate service: "Rejoice, O Pilgrim Throng" (OWC 157).[18] It is scored for congregation, SATB choir, organ, and brass quartet. The introduction uses brass and organ. Material from the introduction is utilized throughout the setting. The disposition of the hymn is as follows:

> st. 1—Congregation sings the cantus firmus. Choir concludes the stanza with a descanting line that is repeated throughout the work. The organ has a four-part setting.
>
> st. 2—Congregation and choir sing the cantus firmus accompanied by a free four-part setting for brass.
>
> st. 3—Choir trebles sing an independent melodic line accompanied by a four-part organ setting.
>
> st. 4—Congregation and choir sing a setting similar to st. 2.
>
> st. 5—Choir sings an independent melodic line accompanied by a march-like organ setting reflecting the concept of the text.
>
> st. 6—Congregation sings the cantus firmus with a trumpet duplicating the melody. Choir trebles sing a descanting line, with another trumpet duplicating the descant. Choir men sing an independent line below the cantus firmus accompanied by the trombones and horn.
>
> st. 7—After an introduction by organ and brass, congregation sings the cantus firmus with a rhythmic accompaniment by the brass and organ, and the choir trebles add a soaring descant.

What a fitting conclusion to the 21 years that Charles Ore, the Concordia Singers, and I spent working together!

APPENDIX A
Choral Settings of Psalms by Charles Ore

OWC #	TITLE	VOICING	PUBLISHER
OWC 13	"Psalm 47"	Unison voices	OWC
OWC 22	"Psalm 1"	SAB	OWC
OWC 23	"Psalm 4"	SAB	OWC
OWC 24	"Psalm 23"	SAB	OWC
OWC 25	"Psalm 25"	SAB	OWC
OWC 82	"Psalm 31"	SATB, organ, and congregation	OWC
OWC 98	"Psalm 96"	SATB, timpani, and brass	OWC
OWC 99	"Psalm 117"	Unison voices and keyboard	OWC

Note: Psalm paraphrases are also used in "Brother James' Air/The Ash Grove" (OWC 103) and "The Lord Has Done Great Things for Me" (OWC 212).

APPENDIX B
Hymn Settings by Charles Ore

OWC #	TUNE	TITLE	PUBLISHER
OWC 66	FINLANDIA	"Be Still, My Soul"	OWC

A hymn concertato for SATB choir, congregation, organ, and instruments

OWC 69	NUN KOMM, DER HEIDEN HEILAND	"Savior of the Nations, Come"	OWC

A hymn concertato for SATB choir, congregation, brass, and organ

OWC 79	ADESTE FIDELES	"Oh, Come, All Ye Faithful"	APH

A festival processional for congregation, choirs, and instruments

OWC 101	IN DULCI JUBILO	"Now Sing We, Now Rejoice"	APH

A festival processional for congregation, choirs, and instruments

OWC 102	SONNE DER GERECHTIGKEIT	"At the Lamb's High Feast We Sing"	OWC

A hymn concertato for SATB choir, congregation, instruments, and organ

OWC 103	BROTHER JAMES' AIR	"Brother James' Air/ The Ash Grove"	OWC

A hymn concertato for SATB choir, congregation, flute, brass, and organ

OWC 103	THE ASH GROVE	"Brother James' Air/ The Ash Grove"	OWC

A hymn concertato for SATB choir, congregation, flute, brass, and organ

OWC 104   THE KING OF GLORY   "The King of Glory Comes"   OWC
A hymn concertato for SATB choir, congregation, diverse instruments, and keyboard

OWC 122   DIADEMATA   "Crown Him with Many Crowns"   OWC
A hymn concertato for SATB choir, congregation, brass, and organ

OWC 156   ST. ANNE   "Our God, Our Help in Ages Past"   CPH
A hymn alternation for SATB choir, descanting instrument, congregation, and keyboard

OWC 157   MARION   "Rejoice, O Pilgrim Throng"   CPH
A hymn concertato for SATB choir, congregation, brass, and organ

OWC 173   WIE SCHÖN LEUCHTET   "O Morning Star, How Fair and Bright"   CPH
A hymn concertato for SATB choir, brass, solo trumpet or oboe, congregation, and organ

OWC 174   O GROSSER GOTT   "O God of God, O Light of Light"   CPH
A hymn concertato for SATB choir, congregation, brass, and organ

OWC 177   DEN SIGNEDE DAG   "O Day Full of Grace"   OWC
A hymn concertato for SATB choir, congregation, brass, and organ

OWC 181   OLD HUNDREDTH   "Praise God in His Temple"   OWC
An anthem for SATB choir, congregation, brass, and organ

OWC 208   ENGELBERG   "When in Our Music God Is Glorified"   OWC
A hymn concertato for SATB choir, congregation, brass, and organ

OWC 212   REUNION   "The Lord Has Done Great Things Indeed"   OWC
A hymn concertato for SATB choir, congregation, brass, timpani, and organ

OWC 228   PUTNAM   "O Splendor of God's Glory Bright"   OWC
A hymn concertato for SATB choir, descant, instruments or handbells, congregation, and organ

OWC 248   (no tune name)   "God Separated Day from Night"   (not publ.)
Four-verse hymn for organ and congregation

OWC 264   WOJTKIEWIECZ   "Rise, Shine, You People"   (not publ.)
A hymn concertato for SATB choir, congregation, trumpet, and organ

OWC 265   WESTMINSTER   "Christ Is Made   (not publ.)
           ABBEY   the Sure Foundation"

A hymn concertato for SATB choir (optional quartet, duet, or soloist), congregation, brass quintet, timpani, and organ

APPENDIX C
Additional Choral Compositions by Charles Ore

OWC #	TITLE	VOICING	PUBLISHER
1	"Scattered by Sin"	Unison voices and keyboard	OWC
39	"He Lives Forevermore"	Treble voices and instruments	APH
41	"Open Our Hearts and Minds, O Lord"	Unison voices and keyboard	OWC
57	"Gloria in Excelsis Deo"	SATB and keyboard	OWC
58	"Glory to God"	SATB, brass, timpani, and keyboard	OWC
68	"Beloved I Adore You"	SB and keyboard	OWC
70	"Oh, Sing for Joy"	Unison voices, percussion, and organ	OWC
80	"O Come, Lord Jesus"	Unison voices and keyboard	OWC
86	"O Come, Lord Jesus, Come"	Unison voices and congregation	OWC
100	"Father, the Time Has Come"	SATB, soloists, brass, keyboard, and congregation	OWC
106	"The Hand of the Lord"	SATB	OWC
123	"Omnes Learned Doctora"	Unison voices and keyboard	OWC
127	"My Crown of Creation"	SATB and organ	MSM
155	"Concordia, Concordia"	Unison voices and keyboard	OWC
175	"There Is a Green Hill Far Away"	SATB, claves, handbells, organ, optional flute, and congregation	CPH
176	"This Is My Son"	SATB, trumpet, organ, and congregation	CPH

| 179 | "Winter Night Gives Birth to Day" | Congregation and Choir | OWC |
| 180 | "A Time and a Purpose" | SATB, congregation, and organ | CPH |

Notes

1. Many of these pieces may still be obtained from Augsburg Publishing House (APH), Concordia Publishing House (CPH), or MorningStar Music Publishers (MSM). OWC works may be obtained from Organ Works Corporation (2523 Bluff Road, Seward, NE, 68434), or Concordia University Nebraska Archives (800 North Columbia, Seward, NE, 68434).

2. Irene Beethe, "Charles W. Ore: From 'My' Perspective" (master's thesis, Concordia University Wisconsin, 2006).

3. Charles W. Ore, accompanying booklet, *From My Perspective 2*, Organ Works Corporation CD (1995). Ore's four CDs are available from Organ Works Corporation (2523 Bluff Road, Seward, NE, 68434); Concordia Publishing House (1–3 only); Amazon; and CD Baby; or on Spotify and iTunes.

4. Inter-Lutheran Commission on Worship, *Lutheran Book of Worship* (Minneapolis: Augsburg, and Philadelphia: Board of Publication, Lutheran Church in America, 1978); Commission on Worship of The Lutheran Church—Missouri Synod, Lutheran Worship (St. Louis: Concordia, 1982)

5. Paul Bunjes, "A Mighty Fortress Is Our God: A Chorale Concertato Based on Historical Settings for Congregation, Choir, Organ, and Three Trumpets" (St. Louis: Concordia, 1957).

6. Appendix A to this essay lists Ore's psalm compositions.

7. "At the Lamb's High Feast" is included on the CD *From My Perspective 4*, Organ Works Corporation (2002).

8. An organ version of the introduction to "At the Lamb's High Feast" is included in *11 Compositions for Organ*, set 4 (St. Louis: Concordia, 1989).

9. Appendix B to this essay lists Ore's compositions based on hymn tunes.

10. "Brother James' Air/The Ash Grove" is included on the CD *From My Perspective 4*.

11. "Now Sing We Now Rejoice" is included on the CD *From My Perspective 2*.

12. "Our God, Our Help in Ages Past" is included on the CD *From My Perspective*, Organ Works Corporation CD (1992). Grant Peters is featured on the trumpet part.

13. "O Morning Star, How Fair and Bright" is included on the CD *From My Perspective 2*. Kermit Peters is featured on the oboe part.

14. Appendix C to this essay lists Ore's additional choral compositions.

15. "A Time and a Purpose" is included on the CD *From My Perspective 4*.

16 "This Is My Son" is included on the CD *From My Perspective 2*.

17 "My Crown of Creation" is included on the CD *From My Perspective*, Organ Works Corporation (1991).

18 "Rejoice, O Pilgrim Throng" is included on the CD *From My Perspective 3*, Organ Works Corporation (1995).

Improvisation, Composition, and Charles

STEVEN EGLER

For a number of years I had been curious about improvising at the organ. Like so many of us organists, I had attended quite a few improvisation workshops given by luminaries in our profession and had always come away full of energy and determination that "I could do this." There was always one problem: when I got home and started to apply these various approaches to my own improvisations, I usually found myself "dead in the water." Result: giving up once again. I'm not saying that I was looking for an easy fix to the art of improvisation, but I was lost when it came to applying a certain methodology, even after these various workshops. Most of these people were very good improvisers, but to me they seemed more involved in (and maybe even distracted by) demonstrating what *they*—as improvisers—could do, rather than teaching *us* how we might do it *ourselves*.

I was young enough, then, to be open still to study or, at least, to be exposed to yet another system of improvising. I never saw myself as having the ability or desire to improvise a symphony as the crowning point of a recital: it was enough of a challenge to play a composed symphony for organ, i.e., by Louis Vierne, Charles-Marie Widor, or César Franck.

By "young enough," I mean I'd already been teaching organ for about 15 years at Central Michigan University (CMU). (This would be somewhere around 1990.) Occasionally I had been asked by students about teaching them improvisation, but I was at a loss to help these students. I also saw how improvisation could have been a useful tool in my church position, but I was always very self-conscious about something going terribly wrong and being embarrassed beyond belief. Sound familiar?

At that time, the Greater Lansing Chapter of the American Guild of Organists was sponsoring an annual church music workshop in January of each year. The annual program featured someone in the profession who gave workshops and then led a festival service later that same day. About 25 years ago, Charles W. Ore was the guest. I was intrigued when I saw his name on the list, because I had heard about his improvisational skills and I knew of his very early compositions for organ. I decided to attend the workshop that particular year and "see what this Ore guy was all about."

Much of the focus that day was on various types of improvisations at the organ, and there were many demonstrations by Charles himself. I recall immediately his sense of humor, his hearty laugh, an almost laissez-faire approach to improvising, and his "can-do" philosophy. Not that he was loose or unprofessional about it: he was being honest with his approach and was always encouraging us that *we* could do it, too.

Then, at some point, he'd done enough demonstrating and exhibiting that what he was talking about could really work. Guess what? He asked for volunteers to give it a try. Have you ever been to an improvisation workshop where the leader asks for volunteers? Amazing how we all wither on the vine and become invisible!

I don't recall who volunteered to try it first, but I *do* remember that I was *not* the first one on the bench. Basically, I was a chicken. After one or two others, I did volunteer, and I recall being given VENI, EMMANUEL as the tune to work with. Charles gave very precise instructions: simple accompaniment, no pedal, playing the melody as is, and maintaining boundaries for the tune and the extent of the accompaniment. He sat right there on the bench with me the whole time, helping me to maintain control of these very basic musical components, emphasizing the importance of being mindful of the *form* of the improvisation. In this case—or any case where a tune is involved—the form is automatically dictated. Our challenge is to stick with it and not stray.

I came away from that session energized, fully equipped with a few tips, and full of confidence from Charles' "can-do" philosophy. Yes, I can do this!

I was mesmerized and attracted to Charles' approach to improvisation. He was not hung up on chordal progressions and the like, and he approached accompaniments from a totally different standpoint: figuration, consistency, and rhythm. He emphasized that variety results from cantus firmus migration, interludes, registration, and so on. Everything he discussed and applied in that workshop seemed very doable and practical.

A slight fast-forward: I had applied for a sabbatical leave from CMU to take place in the spring semester of 1994 to study with Russell Saunders at the Eastman School of Music in Rochester, NY. Russell and I had discussed this for many months and CMU had agreed to this sabbatical, as had Russell himself. However. Russell died unexpectedly in December 1992.

Needless to say, I was devastated. Not only was this a personal loss for me—I had known Russell for many years, having been introduced to him by my teacher, Robert Glasgow—but also I realized immediately what a huge loss it was to our profession. Realizing also that my sabbatical to study with Russell had gone up in smoke, I started to explore what I might do to substitute that leave with something else that was equally credible for a sabbatical from CMU.

I don't know exactly when it came to me, but I started to configure a scenario of going to Nebraska, of all places, to study improvisation with Charles Ore at Concordia in Seward. Why not? I had also met George Ritchie and Quentin Faulkner (then both organ professors at the University of Nebraska–Lincoln) at conventions and conferences, and I considered that working with them as well might be a valid option to round out my sabbatical. I had a full package for a sabbatical and proceeded with my revised proposal.

Ultimately, all three of these distinguished organists, scholars, and pedagogues agreed to take me on as a student during the winter semester of 1995, and CMU approved my revised sabbatical request. I was thrilled! I studied contemporary and Baroque repertoire with George Ritchie and audited his organ literature class; studied mostly

Baroque repertoire and styles with Quentin Faulkner; and studied improvisation with Charles Ore up the road in Seward.

Sabbatical, winter of 1995: Nebraska! A jackpot: Charles Ore, Quentin Faulkner, and George Ritchie!

To this day, I consider this experience during the first four-plus months of 1995 to be one of the most enlightening and stimulating periods of my professional career. I worked with three master teachers who were wonderful people and fabulous musicians and organists. Again, I had hit a jackpot.

Charles' teaching from week to week was just like the workshops that I had attended, except that the intense, weekly, two-hour lessons with him were no comparison to that small amount of time with him in the workshop. Realize that I was in my mid-40s at this time and very nervous about approaching this new aspect of the art of playing the organ. Charles was the perfect person for me at that time.

Lessons would always begin with a little bit of chitchat that always served to relax me and prepare me to dig into the lesson. "How's your week been down the road at UNL?" "Are you getting enough time to practice?" "How's life?"

Then off we'd go. I'd have my prepared improvisations ready for him, feeble as they were, and my carefully prepared notebook of possibilities to play for him. Not once do I recall him ever saying, "That's crazy. Why did you do *that*?" This was an amazing thing for me: to realize that improvisation could be so objective and not so subjective. He always made lemonade out of lemons, *my* lemons!

Some improvisation teachers have their pat phrases, such as, "Salvation is just a half step away!" Charles Ore just kept on keeping on. If I recall him saying anything, it was, "Let's try your way, but with this little change." Meanwhile, he would demonstrate to me how what I had valiantly tried to do might be approached both differently and more easily and sensibly.

There was a lot of me-off-the-bench, Charles-on-the-bench—like any normal organ lesson; but with improvisation, it was more of a back-and-forth experience. He would demonstrate, but then he would expect me to give it a try right away. This is what worked with his teaching style, and I felt that it was really "hands on" as a result.

There was never time to be intimidated or insecure, because the lessons were conducted at lightning speed. (I was always exhausted afterwards because of the intensity of the sessions!)

One other thing before I describe Charles' approach to teaching improvisation: we were most fortunate to use the large Schlicker organ at St. John's Lutheran Church in Seward, where his wife Connie was then the director of music and organist. This was also, from what I recall, a campus church, where organ students from Concordia performed degree recitals and the college choirs performed from time to time.

Charles' approach to improvisation begins with the following guidelines in mind, all of which I use with my own students to this very day, as well as in workshops that I have presented. What follows is a brief basic outline or tutorial of Charles Ore's approach to improvisation.

Guidelines for Basic Improvisation: À la Charles W. Ore

Why Use Cantus Firmus-Based Improvisations?

- It is the most useful type of improvisation to the church musician, because we are always working with hymn tunes.
- The tune is a "given": you do not have to make up (improvise) this.
- Key and harmony are also "givens."
- Form is—mostly—predetermined by the structure of the tune.

Tips

- Always establish boundaries (the electric-fence concept): this is the most difficult thing to achieve.
- Decide on your accompaniment pattern and stick with it: range, intervals, rhythm.
- Practice the pattern alone.
- Decide on your "outline" or form before you begin to improvise and stick with it.
- Practice counting aloud as you do this.

- Determine whether the tune modulates and if it will be necessary to do this in your accompaniment.
- Practice this, hands separately.
- Practice simple transposition: same notes, different key signatures. Then work your way gradually toward other keys.
- Practice improvising as regularly as you practice your repertoire.

Variables
- Tempo;
- Registration;
- Meter;
- Mode: major to minor; minor to major;
- Function or use of a piece in the worship service: short prelude or interlude, hymn introduction, and so on;
- Articulation—*legato* vs. detached; and
- Technique—work with styles within which you feel most comfortable.

Accompaniment
Left hand (LH) then right hand (RH) for each of the following:
- Play one note, ascending and descending, within a one-octave scale: quarter note, two eighths, triplets.
- Play thirds on the one-octave scale: quarter note, two eighths, triplets.
- Start to combine rhythms for variety.
- Change directions so that you are not always playing the scalar pattern.
- Play sixths (use two hands or one) on the one-octave scale, and play thirds (two hands), using the same rhythms as this section's first two parts above. Play the tune in the pedal.
- Play thirds and sixths with both hands on the one-octave scale. Play the tune in the pedal.

Tune or Cantus Firmus

Always practice with hands separately and then with the feet. Sometimes it is handy to be able to play the tune in all voices together!

- Practice the tune—RH, LH, then pedal—in continuous phrases.
- Practice the tune—RH, LH, then pedal—in separated phrases (with interludes).
- Practice migration of the tune: pedal to LH, repeat; LH to RH, repeat; and so forth.
- Practice the tune with simple embellishments: passing tones, upper and lower neighbor tones.

Simple "Outline" or Form

- Hymn introduction—first phrase: tune in RH, detached thirds in LH; fourth phrase: harmonization as-is from hymnal.
- Prelude:
  - Continuous phrases in the tune, with an accompaniment of single notes or thirds on the one-octave scalar pattern;
  - Separated phrases in the tune: tune in LH, sixths in RH;
  - Migration of the tune—prelude; first phrase: tune in LH, thirds in RH; interlude to exchange positions; second phrase: tune in RH, thirds in LH; interlude; and so on.
- Toccata

  RH plays descending broken-chord figuration, with tune in LH, pedal at cadence points:
  - Eighth-note triplets in the key of G major, with added chord tones: G-D-C / G-C-D and so on.
  - Sixteenth-note quadruplets: G-D-C-G / G-D-C-G and so on.
  - Sixteenth-note sextuplets: G-D-C-G-C-D and so on.
    - The use of added chord tones is always a possibility: 4th, 6th, 9th (2nd).

- LH mirroring the RH figuration—broken-chord patterns that reflect the basic harmony of the hymn tune or chordal pattern of the hymn; consider also adding chord tones: 4th, 6th, 9th (2nd).
- Migration of the tune between the pedal and LH and RH.

Of course, one of the most difficult aspects of this process was becoming adept at playing the hymn-tune melody in the pedal. Consider some of the great composers who use this technique: J. S. Bach, Johann Pachelbel, Felix Mendelssohn, Johannes Brahms, Paul Hindemith (Sonata III), Hugo Distler, and Helmut Walcha. Charles' simple reason for developing this technique of playing the tune in the pedal was that it liberated both hands, instead of just one, to play more elaborate accompaniments against the pedal melody.

As I mentioned above, my improvisation lessons were once a week. Mind you, I was practicing and preparing for a total of three lessons a week: one hour with Ritchie (mainly contemporary repertoire, Leo Sowerby's *Symphony*, and Bach as well), one hour with Faulkner (all Bach and some pre-Bach music), and a two-hour lesson with Ore. I was also auditing Ritchie's wonderful organ literature class two mornings a week and attending the organ studio class on Monday afternoons, both at the University of Nebraska–Lincoln. It was a very full week, indeed.

After Charles and I were finished with the niceties of how our respective weeks had gone, he wanted to hear my assignment. Needless to say, I was always nervous and anxious yet eager to play my little improvisations for him and to hear his usually generous comments about my product for the week's lesson. As I said above, he was always quick to comment but never—I say *never*—negative about what I had done. Rather, he always had fairly simple solutions as to how I might approach things differently. He did not say anything along the lines of, "This might make it better." That was not in his make-up as a teacher. It was always taking the Play-Doh of my improvisation and shaping it in a different way. I believe that this alone was Charles' true gift as a teacher: there was never intimidation or subjectivity used. He always encouraged me to keep trying, ro keep looking for different options or possibilities, and thus I was stimulated to keep searching, to keep practicing, and to keep giving it another go.

I had never been so much immersed in practicing and preparing improvisations for such learned ears on a regular basis, and I learned *very quickly* that it is a practiced art. Most people (and most students, as I've discovered) believe that improvisation is something that happens spontaneously.

Like the art of jazz, there are boundaries of form, harmony, texture, and rhythm (this can vary, of course) that all center around the given cantus firmus or melody. Jazz, however, relies more strongly than improvisation on harmony as a structural element, unless the melody is given: melody and harmony are wedded together.

In a certain sense, Charles' approach did not rely as heavily on harmony except in a broad sense: it is all driven by the melodic elements. Considering the guidelines outlined above, Charles was most insistent—and I repeat, *most insistent*—upon establishing the various boundaries for the improvisation.

First, controlling the accompaniment in a formulaic fashion was most difficult. That is, if the boundary set was to keep the accompaniment within the octave compass, *keep it within the octave compass. No exceptions.* Even when the shape of the accompaniment started to change a bit, maintain the octave compass in the accompaniment.

Second, when the improvisation began to expand in a formal sense via the use of interludes between phrases of the hymn tune, get in the habit of counting aloud. If you established eight quarter-note beats as the length of your interludes, *play no more and no less than eight beats when the phrase of the hymn tune is finished.* Many times I recall Charles counting aloud: "1 – 2 – 3 – 4 – 5 – 6 – 7 – 8," both while I was attempting an improvisation as well as when he himself was demonstrating for me. "1 – 2 – 3 – 4 – 5 – 6 – 7 – 8." It still rings in my head and in my ears.

Why is this so important? No matter what form or scope your improvisation takes on, it is essential to maintain a good balance between those sections *with* the tune against those sections *without* the tune. For examples, study the mature chorales of Bach, mainly the 18 Leipzig chorales and the *Clavierübung*, part 3.

Third, I learned that registration—more appropriately, "sound"—was extremely important to one being inspired to develop an improvisation as a whole. Soft sounds, whether they were beautiful flute stops or mushy strings, were just as important as a large sound in order to take an improvisation to the next level of refinement.

An anecdote: St. John's church had recently added a big reed stop, Festival Trumpet 8', before my period of study with Charles Ore, and frequently Charles would reach over while I was playing and add that stop to a full-bodied registration. As best my memory can recall, Charles would say (with that familiar twinkle in his eye), "Let's see what this might do, if it might 'help.'" Of course, yours truly was always trying to underplay my improvisations and not to burden the rest of the church with my creations. What was interesting—and fun—was that the Festival Trumpet always made a difference: a difference for the better. Charles, of course and once again, knew exactly what he was doing, especially with that Festival Trumpet, and I sure am glad that the church invested in that wonderful stop!

I recall one lesson early on in the semester when Charles had received a recently published copy of his *11 Compositions for Organ*, set 6 (1995). This collection included settings of hymns for Advent, Christmas, and Epiphany. He asked me if I'd like to hear these compositions, and of course I said yes. He proceeded to play all of the 11 pieces for me on the Wicks organ in the choral rehearsal room at Concordia. (The church was not available that day.) He briefly described how he had approached each of the various hymn tunes. By this point in my work with him, I was able to see how his various approaches to improvisation had come to fruition in these published compositions. This particular set was a tutorial on his compositional style, especially in regard to his treatment of the cantus firmus (CF). The pieces may be described as follows:

"The King Shall Come" (CONSOLATION)—CF in soprano embellished.

"Come, O Long-Expected Jesus" (JEFFERSON)—CF in soprano embellished and with extended interludes.

"Oh, Come, Oh, Come, Emmanuel" (Veni, Emmanuel)—migrating CF soprano to bass/pedal, closing with classic toccata figuration.

"Away in a Manger" (Cradle Song)—CF in soprano with extended interludes; the Latin rhythm is common to both this piece and the next.

"Away in a Manger" (Cradle Song)—cloning of no. 4, perhaps with CF in soprano with extended interludes; same rhythm as no. 4.

"Away in a Manger" (Away in a Manger)—CF in pedal; development of a secondary theme beginning in m. 3; extended interludes.

"Lo, How a Rose Is Growing" (Es ist ein Ros)—CF in pedal; again, development of a secondary theme beginning in m. 1; extended interludes.

"Of the Father's Love Begotten" (Divinum mysterium)—CF in tenor; rhythm of original chant adapted to 6/8 meter.

"Let All Together Praise Our God" (Lobt Gott, ihr Christen)—embellished CF in soprano with extended interludes.

"Hark! The Herald Angels Sing" (Mendelssohn)—fragmented CF in alto and highly embellished with interludes; free fantasy.

"O Morning Star, How Fair and Bright" (Wie schön leuchtet)—CF in pedal; secondary theme beginning in m. 1; extensive interludes.

   Note that four of the compositions have the CF in the pedal (nos. 3, 6, 7, and 11), six have the CF in the soprano (nos. 1, 2, 3, 4, 5, and 9), one has the CF in the alto and is more of a free-fantasy approach (no. 10), and one has the CF in the tenor (no. 8). All of these settings employ interludes of varying lengths, and some have highly developed secondary themes that are related to the cantus firmus.

That same day in 1995, Charles inscribed the title page of set 6:

This copy for Steve Egler

Charles W. Ore

March 1995

May these compositions evoke pleasant memories associated with the Winter of '95.

Keep alive the tradition of improvisation!

Speaking of published compositions, his subsequent sets 7–9 (2002–2012) include a handful of pieces that had been out of print for some time. How wonderful! Pieces that were part of his various hymn concertatos are now extracted as stand-alone organ compositions: MARION, set 7, and WIE SCHÖN LEUCHTET, set 9. His beautiful setting of STILLE NACHT for organ and oboe has been arranged for solo organ in set 8. Large-scale fantasies include EIN FESTE BURG (originally published in 1990) in set 8 and KOMM, HEILIGER GEIST, HERRE GOTT (originally published in 1975) in set 9.

It was also Charles' habit frequently to discuss how his formal compositions began their lives (at that time; he may have changed his approach by now), usually on an electronic keyboard that could automatically display and print out his music as he improvised it. At that time in 1995, this entire process was totally amazing to me. What I learned later was that what Charles produced on the keyboard and thus on the display screen was pretty much perfect: even more amazing! All he had to do was to make minor changes and print out the finished composition.

All composers approach their art in different ways, yet many of them use the piano or a keyboard as the vehicle to put on paper the final product that they envision. Modern technology has certainly made the process of composing easier—putting notes on staffs on paper. Some, I know, still use the "old-fashioned" way of handwritten notation on manuscript paper.

What is important to realize about Charles Ore's approach is that he is an improviser first: a great and extremely talented improviser who conceives music in his mind and in his hands and feet. It then comes out perfectly as a finished composition, as he has evidenced on many occasions.

This leads me to make a brief observation about sets 1 and 2 of *11 Compositions for Organ* and about the two above-mentioned hymn fantasies (Komm, Heiliger Geist and Ein feste Burg). There are no time signatures in either Komm, Heiliger Geist or set 1 (except for one: Allein Gott). On the other hand, Ein feste Burg does have time signatures, but they are at best a nod toward more conventional musical notation and include many irregular meters. For example, m. 1 is 15/16 and the next measure is 12/16. Page 4 has a series of measures that are 15/16, 10/16, 8/16, and 12/16, and page 5 has several measures thus: 7/16, 9/16, 6/16, 7/16. Of the 11 compositions in set 2, six are *with* time signatures and 5 are *without*.

Another characteristic in set 1 is Charles' use of an unusual style of notation that indicates length for long note values by means of a line or lines following the note or notes. This line indicates how long the note is to be held (in relation to the other voices) and is used in place of specific note values. This technique serves his free compositional style very well, since the other voices then continue at their own, individual speeds. There is no tyranny of the bar line restricting these compositions, which were obviously born as improvisations that were written down on paper.

It is easy to see that Charles Ore attempted to keep his early published compositions as close as possible to what his improvisations must have been like. He did, however, evolve to being just a bit more conventional, both with basic rhythms and with how those basic rhythms adapted to a particular meter.

We can only thank the Great Provider that our technology is able to accommodate Charles' music and translate it into a finished product on paper, both in the early compositions and in the more recent works.

At a certain point in my study with Ore, we were developing certain material on a handful of hymn tunes over a few weeks' time. Unbeknownst to me (in my naiveté), Charles was gently guiding me towards composing. I use this term *very* lightly and with the greatest of humility! During one lesson, as we were working on New Britain ("Amazing Grace"), he suggested that I might "put my improvisation down on paper" and start to solidify my thoughts about what was developing as a set of variations. I looked at him in utter amazement and asked, "Do you mean the 'C' word?" ("C" meaning "compose.") He got that familiar and omnipresent twinkle in his eye and answered with a nod of his head. I'll never forget that moment. Not that I saw myself as a budding composer at the age of 45. Far from it! But *he* had enough confidence in me to encourage me to solidify my musical thoughts and improvisation on paper.

Let me say that the process of writing down on paper what had heretofore been in my head *was not easy.* It is one thing to return to an improvisation-in-progress on a day-to-day basis; it is quite another to make one's ideas concrete in the form of notes on the page.

I would like to add that my composing process was entirely old school. I had gobs of manuscript paper and good pens and pencils. Plus, my notation was fairly neat and readable. I did not have access to or the ability to use technology to transfer the improvisations to readable notation. As a result, I felt a bit like the composers of yesteryear who put everything down in a laborious fashion.

It was a good exercise.

I share all of this with our readers because I know that this is Charles Ore's process. Anyone who has ever heard him improvise knows the perfection with which he issues his musical and inspiring music, seemingly off of the top of his head. It's no wonder that his printed music comes out in such concise and organized form, as evidenced in his many compositions, especially his nine sets of *11 Compositions for Organ* (1971–2012). (Note: set 10 is forthcoming in 2017.)

The memories of my study with Charles Ore are indelibly imprinted in my brain forever. Perhaps Charles would be embarrassed to know that I was so impressionable as a middle-aged person and musician, and that I hung on every word that he shared with me. That was well over 20 years ago, but my experience with Charles (as well as with Quentin and George) represents a milestone in my life and career. Each one of these teachers was a master pedagogue in his own, special way, and I had been teaching long enough to see how each one of their individual styles worked with me.

I left Nebraska with a renewed outlook on the greater perspective of being a musician and a teacher. I felt freed from my own, self-imposed restrictions: more positive and confident about performing in general.

The entire exercise of learning and applying improvisation to my own portfolio of abilities was something beyond description. I became more studious and diligent as I learned and relearned repertoire. Why? Much—not all, however—keyboard music, in particular, is conceived in improvisation. As I moved further in time from my Nebraska sabbatical, I realized that this was being reflected in how I approached performing and teaching. All of this was for the better!

I owe a huge debt of gratitude to Charles Ore—master teacher, improviser, composer, church musician, humanitarian, mentor, and generous person—for his contagious spirit and knowledge. My life as a person, teacher, and musician changed dramatically after my study with him, and I will be forever grateful to him for that.

Happy 80th birthday, Charles! You deserve every bit of the kudos that will come your way on this momentous occasion in your life. I thank you for your many gifts.

What a Music Publisher Values in a Composer

BARRY L. BOBB

Introduction

First, a couple of disclosures: I have been a big fan of the music of Charles Ore for over 45 years. As an organ student in college I was drawn to his publications, even though I knew nothing about him personally and had never heard him play. There was always a certain freshness and excitement about his compositions. They were unlike any other music I was studying. For my master's degree organ recital in 1978, my wife and I commissioned a new work from Ore, an adagio and fugue on Es ist das Heil. It is a brilliant piece, and each year I still pull out the manuscript around Reformation Day and play it. I had no way of knowing then that within eight years our relationship would enter a new phase.

From 1986 to 2002 I served in various roles at Concordia Publishing House in St. Louis, MO, including director of music and worship. Based on those years, the editor of this Festschrift asked if I might reflect on that period (a time of great creative output from Ore) and on the unique relationship between a publisher and a composer, especially in church music. I hope that these thoughts provide some common ground and lead to understanding and fruitful partnerships between many composers and their publishers and that this makes it easier for aspiring (and sometimes frustrated) composers for the Church.

(By the way, I still have—after all these years—many favorite Ore pieces to which I return on a regular basis, including "A Mighty

Fortress," "I Love to Tell the Story," "Prepare the Royal Highway," "Beautiful Savior," "Come, Holy Ghost," and "Sonata I.")

Second, an acknowledgement: I have been away from the day-to-day operations of church music publishing since 2002. A special word of appreciation goes to Mark Lawson, president of MorningStar Music Publishers, for expanding and updating my perceptions and understanding of the unique partnership of composer and publisher.

The Nature of the Relationship between Publisher and Composer

The nature of the relationship between composers and their publisher is, in some ways, a standard business arrangement. Each person is entering into an agreement with the hope of some possible financial gain, the same as any contract. But the relationship is also unique in many ways. It seeks to be mutually beneficial. Its purpose is to help the other reach personal and professional goals. The relationship must be based on integrity, a bond of trust, and an abiding respect for each other's expertise, for each brings a unique set of skills to the partnership. In *church* music the relationship between composer and publisher is often more personal and deeper, for they share more than common personal goals. They also share a *passion*—a commitment to music as an art, to the organ as an instrument, and to choral music as an idiom. In most cases, they also share a commitment to the Gospel and to the Church. Often both are active members in dynamic congregations. In their shared endeavor they are not so much developing and selling a product to a customer as they are seeking to equip colleagues in music ministry. There is almost always a sense of "we're in this together."

The composer and the publisher also share a *risk*—they are making a living as "creatives" and, as such, putting so much of themselves into their craft and presenting it in a very public marketplace. They are putting who they are "out there" and opening themselves up to public critique and to the analysis of others, which is often rewarding but can be a painful experience especially in this age of social media. Both have their names on the publication. For each, their reputation is intrinsically woven into their shared endeavor.

Let's look at this relationship more closely from the vantage point of the publisher.

A Church Music Publisher Values a Composer Who Is . . .

. . . a church *musician*.

By that I mean that composers, whether professional musicians or not, are those who are *attentive to their craft.* They approach their task with both great care and ingenuity. They know what has happened before and what is happening now. They have a thorough awareness of the rich and broad heritage of the Church's music. But at the same time they are not hidebound by tradition; they work to build on what they have been given. Certainly throughout his life of composing Ore has worked with traditional church music forms. In reflecting on his oeuvre he maintains that "I have tried to develop a style of writing cantus firmus compositions indigenous to American culture yet *reflective of historic traditions* that have been used by composers of organ literature for hundreds of years."[1]

At the same time he has always kept up with what other composers are doing, even those in the wider musical world, often noting that "the present time is always of the most interest."[2] With ties to both historic and current music, Ore has been able to explore his own musical personality and create a truly distinctive style, one that is yet faithful to the Lutheran tradition. Many of our most useful church composers today follow a similar path. They study the historic literature and strive to write interesting, engaging music. They are driven by an unflagging zeal for excellence, even in simplicity. Finding that right balance between tradition and self-expression and self-exploration is probably one of the most important issues for church musicians and for the institutions that train them.

A big part of "craft" is *discernment*. The best composers use only the highest quality materials both in terms of texts and tunes. They not only have an appreciation for language but also see words as a part of the firstfruits offering the musicians of the Church are making in every worship service. Ore himself has said that the "words are everything."[3] The music grows naturally out of the texts. Discernment also looks inward. A good composer is one capable of aggressive self-critique. One of my early music theory professors, Paul Bunjes, always told his students, "Composers can judge the quality of their work in a given day by how full their wastebasket is at the end." Church composers are at their best when they offer their best.

"Craft" also implies a continuing *determination to get better*, a relentless drive that does not wane as the years go by: "I grow older, always learning" (Solon, 638 BC–558 BC). Publishers are drawn to those composers who take advantage of professional growth opportunities and organizations and demonstrate an ongoing maturing of their personal style. This is not an absolute, but it helps if the composers are also *active church musicians*. They make music in their congregation and love doing so! This solidifies a bond with those who may use their compositions and helps them to see the gaps in the current literature, both in organ and choral repertoire. Many successful church composers bring the same curiosity, courage, playfulness, energy, and determination to both tasks. They bring vitality to all parts of the Church's heritage and repertoire.[4] Fulfilling both roles also enables the church composer to understand the realities of a parish musician's life (both for volunteers and professionals) and the pressures of preparing for weekly services.

A Church Music Publisher Values a Composer Who Is . . .

. . . a *church* musician.

By this I mean that their love of music is matched by their *love for the Church*. They are not so much interested in the *business* of music as they are the *ministry* of music. Ours is a very different world! The Church's musicians see themselves in a certain light. They are not performers as much as they are *servants*:

1. They are *servants of the Word* and are unabashed about Christian doctrine. When describing the craft of the church composer, Ore puts as much weight on theology as he does on musical knowledge, and he is alarmed at some creeping deficiencies when surveying the current scene.[5] He describes this sacred trust most beautifully as " the weekly wrapping and unwrapping of eternal truths."

   The composer, using elements such as melody, rhythm, form, harmony, texture, dynamics, performance media, and aesthetics creates/assembles (wraps) a package that need to be opened (performed). . . .They have the skills to assemble a composition that unites words, music, and theology. . . . Others [church musicians] develop skills necessary to unwrap those packages: study scores, understand the obvious and the nuance while gathering and preparing performers and creating great performances.[6]

2. They *serve the Church and her liturgy*. Although there is much great church music that serves the Word well in concert settings, the greater need continues to be music that can enhance the regular weekly services. Whether they are leading God's people in song or offering a musical sacrifice of praise on their behalf, church musicians will always have a need for new compositions.

3. At their best, church musicians—both composers and performers—*serve the people in the pew*, both adults and children. They are more teachers (perhaps even "pastoral musicians") than "artists in residence" and can discern their role in the context of the church's overall ministry. They keep a balance of past and present in their ministry to believers of all ages. They are always looking forward, creating opportunities for young and old to have a genuine role in the worship life of their congregation and giving full expression to their sung prayer and praises.

A Church Music Publisher Values a Composer Who Is . . .

. . . a good communicator.

As in any interpersonal relationship, it is important that both parties are *eager to speak up* and to speak clearly, so that there is a robust exchange of ideas. It works well when composers are willing to offer ideas, to lay out project proposals in advance, to bounce ideas off their publisher before getting too deeply into their composition. Publishers often can quickly evaluate a proposal as valid or feasible or offer ideas to broaden and strengthen the overall usefulness of the work. And given the intricacies of copyright these days, with so many new restrictions on texts and tunes, the publisher can steer a composer away from a choice that is only going to bring frustration.

In addition to speaking up, it is also important that composers be active, *engaged listeners*. This implies not only the early feedback mentioned above but also an openness to hearing what an editor may suggest. A publisher over the years develops a "house style" that works for them and their customers, and that style may be different from the default settings of the computer programs Finale or Sibelius. Fresh eyes and ears most often help to refine a composition. For an organist and choral conductor, nothing is more frustrating than vague or even missing directions on the page. This kind of listening can be difficult to do, especially when composers have invested so much time into their pieces and brought them to a point of closure where they are ready to share it with others. Suddenly some outsider wants to make changes?! But editing is still an important step toward successful publication. In my book-editing days, I would often share with novice authors a chapter from *James A. Michener's Writer's Handbook: Explorations in Writing and Publishing* (still available in a new paperback edition[7]), in which he shows the drafts, original manuscripts, *and editorial changes* in the first chapter of his book *Journey*. The not-too-subtle message to the aspiring author: if James Michener can be edited, so can you!

A Church Music Publisher Values a Composer Who . . .

. . . sweats the details.

These details include the not-so-much-fun realities of deadlines, editorial changes, and the markings a performer needs to bring the composer's piece to life (tempo, articulation, phrasing, registration, dynamics, and so forth). Do not assume that amateur performers will discern the nuances in your composition. Give them as much help as you can so that their performance is what you imagined.

But this also includes the composer gaining a basic understanding of the financial models of church music publishing. There is much competition in church music publishing and, contrary to popular perceptions, the margins are usually very small. There are financial limitations with which only the publisher must deal. Composers make money on every piece they publish. The publisher is not in such a promising position. For many, perhaps only one-half of their publications break even, and from the ones that perform better than average they must pay salaries and benefits, publication costs, promotional and marketing expenses,. and other costs unseen by the average person. There is also the complexity of simultaneously marketing hundreds or thousands of titles in print and the cost of music clinics, keeping up the online catalog and online access, and so on. This is a very complicated business! It is also helpful when novice composers research the niche a particular publisher might occupy and do not waste time (and diminish their own financial prospects) by sending publishers manuscripts that are outside their focus.

A Church Music Publisher Values a Composer Who . . .

> . . . works with the publisher in post-publication activities, especially promotion.

Part of understanding music publishing and building a mutually beneficial relationship with the publisher is understanding the importance of self-promotion (in the best sense of that word) and assisting the publisher in their marketing work as well. The most experienced and successful composers know this. They keep their publisher informed of professional activities and stay on the lookout for joint promotional opportunities. Conversely, they understand the dangers of social media posting and the damage that can be done both to themselves and to their publishing partners. Many composers today do their own recordings. Charles Ore did that in his *From My Perspective* series of CDs. What makes these performances outstanding is that he saw the recording process as a new stage of a continuing creative process in which "each element has been carefully constructed and reconstructed in order to create a precise effect."[8] Now that is dedication to one's craft! Composers today also often maintain their own websites with all the latest information relating to their professional lives. Most church musicians, amateur and professional, enjoy learning more about the people who write the music they love to perform. That growing familiarity leads to more sales.

Conclusion

Of course, all of the above presents the ideal. As in the rest of life, we seldom if ever attain an ideal. We all fall short both as composers and as publishers. But we have great models around us to show us the way and to inspire us to strive for perfection. Charles Ore is one such model. He is a model of:

> a creative, deeply imaginative mind in service to the Word of God, encouraging countless others "to trust their inner musical instincts and to enjoy the process of exploring their own musical personalities";[9]
>
> a composer and cantor for the Church;
>
> a teacher *of* the Church; and
>
> a Christian husband, father, grandfather, colleague, and friend.

So, thank you, Charles, and happy 80th birthday! *Ad multos annos*![10]

Notes

1   Charles W. Ore, accompanying material, From My Perspective, Organ Works Corporation CD (1992); emphasis added.

2   Charles W. Ore, quoted in Brent Nolte, "The Organ Music and Musical Philosophy of Charles W. Ore," The American Organist 37 (March 2003): 66.

3   Charles W. Ore, quoted in Ryan A. Winningham, "Cut from the Same Cloth? Two Perspective on Music for Worship" (senior seminar in music, Hope College, 2003), 2.

4   This is particularly evident in Ore's insightful and thorough chapter on how to accompany northern European hymnody found in Leading the Church's Song, ed. Robert Buckley Farlee and Eric Vollen (Minneapolis: Augsburg Fortress, 1998), 36–60.

5   Charles W. Ore, quoted in Nolte, 70.

6   Charles W. Ore, "Eternal Truths: Wrapped and Rewrapped," in This Is the Feast: Richard Hillert at 80, ed. James Freese (St. Louis: MorningStar , 2004), 69–74.

7   James A. Michener, James A. Michener's Writer's Handbook: Explorations in Writing and Publishing (New York: The Dial Press, 2015; originally published in 1992).

8   Charles W. Ore, accompanying material, From My Perspective (1992).

9   Charles W. Ore, quoted in Nolte, 70.

10 "To many years!" (i.e., many happy returns).

What a Composer Values in a Publisher

KENNETH T. KOSCHE

Barry L. Bobb offers valuable insights from a publisher's perspective in his essay, "What a Music Publisher Values in a Composer." I am pleased to have been invited to contribute to this Charles Ore Festschrift by providing a point-counterpoint essay as a composer. I also am pleased to note that Barry and I shared an excellent publisher–composer relationship—as did Charles Ore and others—during the years in which Barry served in that role at Concordia Publishing House.

In order to provide a counterpoint to Barry's essay, I have elected to use the same headings with "composer" and "publisher" transposed throughout. Every relationship that is fruitful and enduring is two-directional. Ideas and issues travel in both directions freely and regularly. While there is certainly a standard business relationship, the serious composer hopes for a deeper relationship over time based on more than shared revenue. There is no doubt that ideals of musical artistry, theological integrity, and commitment to service of God and of the Church are central to a healthy relationship between composer and publisher. It is a shared bond that transcends the bottom line, yet each party needs to be aware of the success of the other for a fulfilling and sustained relationship, one lived out in the public eye in worship and concert. I concur with Barry that the reputation of each "is intrinsically woven into their shared endeavor." A composer might remain a local phenomenon without the aid of the publisher. A publisher develops and builds a reputation on the basis of materials provided regularly by composers identified with a publishing house—yes, even beyond one publisher, if the composer reaches acclaim among other publishers. The success of one is directly proportional to the other. Yet each brings a different perspective. The following ideas are my take on the relationship. I write from the viewpoint of a practicing parish musician who is a serious church music composer.

A Composer Values a Church Music Publisher Who Is . . .

. . . a church *musician.*

A composer's perspective is primarily one of creating musical and artistic works, though church music composers bring a theological perspective to their craft as well. As an artist, a composer needs to work with people who are also artists, perhaps primarily as performers or, at the least, consumers and appreciators of good music. The more musically skilled the people at the publishing house, the easier it is for each party to work with the other. This includes not only the executive in charge of publishing but also and especially the editors and engravers.

In this technological age, music publishers expect composers to send materials already suitably engraved in such computer applications as Finale or Sibelius. It saves time and money in the editing process, and it is therefore important for a composer to be as facile as possible with the publisher's engraving program. Furthermore, a composer ought to be just as familiar with a publisher's preferred house style, fonts, layout, and the like. It saves the publisher time, and—as is rightly said—"Time is money." Years ago, publishers would pay a small remuneration to a composer for sending in neatly computer engraved pages needing little if any editing. Nowadays, it is virtually expected. Submitting hand manuscripts seems to be a thing of the past. However, when I have taken the effort to notate *exactly* as I wish, I do not enjoy an editor pre-emptorially declaring, "That's not house style!" as an excuse for changing my notation to a way that does not express my intent. It seems reasonable to me to at least discuss our differences of opinion. The more the editor views the work through the eyes of a practicing musician and less as a computer technician, the easier it is to have such a discussion. It may be that I have notated the passage clumsily or incorrectly, and I may need constructive editing. But it frustrates me when I see something of mine appear in print that an editor has changed without apparently understanding the musical reason for notating it my way. This has happened to me only a few times, but I believe it to be totally unnecessary if only the editor thought like a musician, not as a template-wielding computer technician. Worse, one such piece was reprinted in a collection without my knowledge and without correcting the mistake. It is too late to discuss once the piece is in print!

Several publishers have improved my writing by helpfully suggesting ways to amend a piece I have submitted. I recall one instance with particular fondness. The publisher said in effect, "While I will be happy to publish what you have submitted, might you not consider the following ideas?" The publisher's musicianship led to suggesting ideas not readily apparent to me, and the result was a piece of greater appeal than my original. By showing a liking of my piece while simultaneously making valuable suggestions for improvement, the publisher and I found a win-win situation. The piece was improved, and I subsequently held my publisher in higher regard for the shared insight.

A Composer Values a Church Music Publisher Who Is . . .

. . . a *church* musician.

Composers value publishers who are actively involved in the regular worship life of their congregations. Because of their involvement, they may see the need for certain literature. When a composer proposes an idea, it is satisfying if the publisher sees its practical use. There is a need for SATB choral music, perhaps with *divisi* parts, several octaves of handbells, brass quartet, percussion, organ, and congregational response. Not every congregation is equipped to perform it. People who think one must perform *Aïda* every Sunday miss the fact that smaller parishes are generally short the requisite elephants and spear bearers to do so! Knowing which piece to send to which publisher occasionally requires a composer's educated guess. An example from 30 years ago comes to mind. I sent a larger work to one publisher and a simpler arrangement to another. The responses reminded me of "The Three Bears": "too big!" said the one; "too small!" said the other. I switched the pieces, and apparently then they were "just right." Even when the experienced composer tries, it is often difficult to gauge a publisher's needs and desires.

I am grateful that long ago one of my publishers said, "'Simple' need not mean 'simple minded.'" This was not the response of a mere musician. It was the response of a *church* musician. Composers would like publishers to give a serious look at compositions and arrangements that have theological and artistic integrity whether large or small and not disdain simple pieces that are easy to perform— what people euphemistically call "accessible." A publisher might take a chance on something simple because it could serve a segment of the church otherwise bereft of literature due to the lack of personnel or to the skill level of the parish musicians.

Consequently, it is helpful when publishers make known specific needs and provide an adequate time frame for the completion of requested projects. I have often wondered how publishing houses can thrive only upon various yearly unsolicited submissions. Surely, knowing the needs of the Church and the contents of their catalogs to fill these needs, more publishers could make needs known to regular contributors without necessarily signaling acceptance in advance of submission.

Composers of vocal music generally do not prefer a publisher to edit a text, especially an established text. For example, I believe that making a Charles Wesley hymn or some part of the Ordinary subject to the whims of the times regarding "inclusive" or so-called "archaic language" is a perversion. Here the composer bears some responsibility to check out similar publications by the publisher and determine a publishers' literary practice. Publishers who have good theological insight and integrity and who point out problematic places in certain lyrics are an asset. Not every composer chooses texts wisely, but when a wise choice appears to have been made, composers do not like publishers editing established texts (go ahead—ask yourself, "What would Charles Wesley say about it?"), especially when the meaning, the rhythm, and the pointing of the text (word accents) are changed, spoiling the artistry of the music as well.

A Composer Values a Church Music Publisher Who Is . . .

. . . a good communicator.

I rejoice when I receive timely correspondence and responses. A simple acknowledgement—an e-mail is fine with me—that a piece has been received or that a decision about a submission has been made is greatly appreciated. Composers know that publishers have established cycles of receiving, reviewing, accepting or declining, editing, proofing, sending contracts, and the like. It is useful for a publisher to make this information generally known to prospective composers, perhaps on a website. That being said, my greatest frustration is not knowing the status of a piece after a lengthy period of time waiting with no communication from the publisher. Odd occurrences happen, publishers get backed up with work, circumstances intervene. It is simply good business for a composer to get some sort of status report after a reasonable length of time. A composer ought to know, say, by six months if a piece is still under consideration. Any composer understands, "No thank you, but we wish you good luck in finding another publisher for this one." Silence is not helpful. After what I felt was an all-too-lengthy wait years ago, a publisher finally wrote to me, "and you Lutherans don't believe in limbo!" We had a nice personal relationship, and I appreciated the fact that unusual circumstances in this case caused an undue delay. Generally, however, for the sake of both parties, publishers need to communicate acceptances and rejections in a timely fashion. Who knows? Perhaps the piece would be a better fit at a different house.

Every church music publisher I have ever dealt with knows composers send their wares to other publishing houses. Experienced composers know that any publisher can reasonably accept only a few offerings each year from among the many composers who submit manuscripts. For more prolific composers, publishers expect that some manuscripts will be sent to them and some to another and possibly some to yet others. This is not a slight to any publisher, but it is a recognition of the reality that a good catalog cannot contain works by only a few composers. This is one more reason to expect a timely word about acceptance or rejection or a reasonable extension of time for further consideration. A composer should not be kept in doubt as to the status of already-submitted publications. On the other hand, double submitting (sending a composition for consideration to more than one publisher at a time) is a no-no!

A publisher need not offer a rejection critique, especially if the critique could be viewed as hurtful. "We cannot use this piece at this time" is sufficient, or "We already have several arrangements of this tune in our catalog." Composers understand rejections, and they respect publishers who accept some pieces but decline others. It is not the *reason* but the *timeliness* that ultimately matters. If composers think that their pieces are still under consideration after a substantial wait, why would they send even more to the same publisher? Lengthy indecision is a loss for both composer and publisher.

A Composer Values a Church Music Publisher Who . . .

. . . sweats the details.

For this reason, composers should take infinite pains to model their submissions after a specific publisher's house style. That being said, there may be exceptions to this rule. "Modifications" might be a better term. I value the opportunity to present my case in a positive way when something seems to be important to me to be engraved differently. As stated earlier, I sincerely appreciate the opportunity to discuss details when appropriate.

A Composer Values a Church Music Publisher Who . . .

. . . works with the composer in post-publication activities, especially promotion.

I have little to add to Barry's comments in this category except to say that not all composers are well positioned to promote their compositions through workshops and conventions and must rely primarily on their publishers to promote their wares. When requested, complimentary copies for workshops are vital in this endeavor. Happily, most publishers readily reply to reasonable requests.

Occasionally, pieces are placed in the "POP" (permanently out of print) category. Several of mine have suffered that not-uncommon fate. However, I find it embarrassing when asked by someone for a recommended composition of mine, which I give them, only to discover it cannot be located in the publisher's catalog or on the publisher's website. This is a crossover comment from the previous section about good communication between publishers and composers. It would be helpful to be informed of pieces going out of print. Some publishers do this; others do not. Print-on-demand is helpful at times like this by allowing music that's no longer widely in demand—yet possesses qualities a future generation may find attractive—to remain available without undue expense to a publisher. It is helpful to a composer to know when this option is available for previous publications.

Conclusion

Those of us who desire to contribute to the life of the Church and to the enrichment of worship through composing appreciate the opportunity to work with church music publishers who demonstrate integrity and zeal for the same.

Charles Ore has made many fine compositional contributions in his four-score years. We wish him much joy, success, and blessings in Christ in doing so in the future. May his labors continue to be well received and richly blessed now and for generations to come.

"Lead Me in Your Truth and Teach Me"

The Church Musician as Teacher

JEFFREY BLERSCH

Now Hear This![1]

It was the summer of 1989. I was an undergraduate student at Oberlin Conservatory of Music in Oberlin, OH, at the time, studying organ and music education. I loved my time at Oberlin and, to this day, value the marvelous education that I received in that small town in the midst of the Ohio corn fields. I was learning how to be a good organist and how to be an effective teacher. I didn't know it at the time, but both of these areas of study would be strong influences in my future vocation as a church musician and contribute to my interest in leading the song of the Church.

Knowing of my interest in church music, a friend invited me to attend a two-day church music clinic sponsored by Augsburg Fortress held in Worthington, OH. As much as I enjoyed the music of J. S. Bach, and as much as I was fascinated by questions of historic performance practice, I was anxious to explore more vexing issues facing church musicians than the discussion of authentic ornamentation in Bach's *Orgelbüchlein*. It was during these two days that I first encountered the name Charles Ore, heard some of his music, and discovered an approach to the organ that would forever change my perception of the instrument.

One of the reading sessions included selections from Ore's *11 Compositions for Organ*, set 4, newly published at the time by

Concordia Publishing House. The clinician said, "Can you imagine the excitement you'll create by introducing the hymn 'Christ Be My Leader' with this?" She then launched into playing on the 73-rank Schlicker organ—complete with Trompeta Real—Charles' "Fanfare Introduction." My heart was racing—not from the volume, but from the energetic rhythms, percussive articulations, mixed meter, and the rather Olympic open fifths.

Next in the reading session was Ore's setting of "Earth and All Stars" from the same publication. Once again, I was captivated by the rhythms, articulations, and mixed meter. What really stood out to me in this piece, however, were the colorful registrations indicated on the page. Never before had I heard a hymn tune treated on the organ in this unique manner. Needless to say, I was hooked. I came home that day with every Charles Ore book that they had for sale.

As I eagerly began to make my way through this new music, I noticed how specific the registrations were. At first glance, some of them seemed a little odd to me. An 8' and a 1', really? And then couple it to the pedal with a 16'? Who does this? It all seemed a little unorthodox to me, but I quickly became enamored of it. It was through these pieces that I began to realize the enormous role that color, timbre, and texture can play in creating an effective interpretation of a hymn tune.

The next fall I brought Charles' music back with me to First Church (United Church of Christ) in Oberlin, where I was the organist at the time. I remember the smiles that it brought to people's faces and how much they remembered those pieces. They were drawn into the hymns through Charles' interpretations. There it was: Charles was teaching me, and he was teaching the Church through his music. And we didn't even know each other—yet. A long history of tutelage was begun that summer in Worthington, a history that continues to this very day.

"How Clear Is Our Vocation, Lord"

The question "what do you do?" is one that we all encounter many times throughout our lifetime. Perhaps this question is sometimes asked in an effort to make idle chitchat while passing time; in other cases, the person may be genuinely interested in finding out more about our occupation. In either case, when I answer this question by saying that I am a musician, the next questions are usually, "Oh really? What do you play? Do you do country? Classic rock?" My answer is, "I am a church musician." Sometimes this answer is met with passive acceptance in an effort to move the conversation on to another topic; sometimes it is followed by a quizzical look as if to say, "so what exactly does a church musician do?"

I once heard Charles Ore answer this question with another question. "What *don't* we do?" he said, while looking over his glasses with a smile on his face.

It's a good answer. After all, church musicians are performers, conductors, and composers. We are soloists, chamber musicians, and accompanists. We are organizers, planners, and enablers. We coach, recruit, and encourage. We comfort, celebrate, and mourn with those whom we serve. And then we do it all over again, all the while trying to remember to order new choir music, bake something for the Ladies Aid potluck on Sunday, and take out the trash on Friday. But above all else, we are teachers. We teach while we perform, conduct, compose, accompany, plan, and encourage. We are privileged to play a vital role in the apostolic ministry of the Church by proclaiming Christ Crucified through the combination of text with various frequencies, rhythms, timbres, and textures. We do it not for the sake of the art form itself, but rather so that we—the Church—may grow in faith toward Christ and in fervent love toward one another.

This apostolic ministry—teaching—is one of the chief responsibilities of the Church. When Jesus issues the Great Commission, he says that we are to make disciples of all nations by "baptizing them in the name of the Father, and of the Son, and of the Holy Spirit, *teaching* them to observe all that I have commanded you" (Matthew 28:19 ESV; emphasis added). St. Paul writes that "whatever was written in former days was written for our instruction, that through endurance and through the encouragement of the scriptures we might have hope" (Romans 15:4). When Philip asked the Ethiopian eunuch, "Do you understand what you are reading?" the eunuch replied, "How can I, unless someone guides me?" (Acts 8:30–31). The Apology of the Augsburg Confession (XV, 42) puts it this way: "and yet the chief worship of God is to preach the gospel."[2]

What do church musicians teach? They first teach us how to sing. This is so basic yet so very important in our culture. After all, with the exception of a rousing rendition of "Happy Birthday" and possibly joining in singing "The Star-Spangled Banner" at sporting and civic events (and even that is questionable), the concept of communal singing has become rather foreign to many. As a whole, we do not tend to understand the benefits of communal singing and, in some cases, we do not even understand how to go about doing it. The church musician first teaches us the language of music and how to go about making real, authentic music.

One might think that this teaching takes place primarily within the choirs of the Church. While this is partially true, since the choir members are certainly recipients of additional instruction, this teaching reaches everyone in the congregation. When the choirs assume the role of leaders and encouragers of the song, the church musician is teaching the entire congregation through the choir. When church musicians take every opportunity to instill in our children a love for the church's song and how to sing musically, they are teaching the Church to sing. When church musicians lead a hymn from the organ or piano in a vocal manner and draw attention to the text by encouraging proper phrasing with the punctuation, they are teaching the congregation how to sing with meaning. When church musicians lead a hymn in an encouraging, convincing, stylistic, and musical manner, they are teaching the congregation to sing with boldness and confidence.

"Through the Church the Song Goes On"

The church musician teaches us that God's Church sings. The song of the Church belongs to *all* of us because we are a part of the Church. Consider that at the creation of the earth "the morning stars sang together and all the sons of God shouted for joy" (Job 38:7). Consider also that in Revelation, St. John heard "the voice of many angels, numbering myriads of myriads and thousands of thousands, saying with a loud voice, 'Worthy is the lamb who was slain'" (Revelation 5:11–12). These passages are but two of many references to singing found in Scripture, but they do illustrate an important point: that the Church—God's creation—has sung from the very beginning of time and will continue to do so through the end of time. We, God's people, have the marvelous opportunity to participate in this song of the universal, timeless church—right here, right now—on this particular date and in this particular place.

Dietrich Bonhoeffer, states it this way:

> "O Sing to the Lord a new song," the Psalter calls out to us again and again. It is the Christ hymn, new every morning, which a community living together begins to sing in the early morning, the new song that is sung by the whole community of faith in God on earth and in heaven. We are called to join in the singing of it. It is God who has prepared one great song of praise throughout eternity, and those who enter God's community join in this song. . . . It is the voice of the church that is heard in singing together. It is not I who sing, but the church. However, as a member of the church, I may share in its song. Thus all true singing together must serve to widen our spiritual horizon. It must enable us to recognize our small community as a member of the great Christian church on earth and must help us willingly and joyfully to take our place in the song of the church with our singing, be it feeble or good.[3]

When we pray in the Litany in Evening Prayer for "those who toil, those who sing," it is important to realize that we are not praying for the choir. (Although I know many church choirs who would welcome prayers on their behalf.) Rather, we are praying for the Church, for all "here present who await from the Lord great and abundant mercy,"[4] because Christ's Church sings.

"To God and to the Lamb I Will Sing"

Through leadership of the song of the Church, the church musician teaches us that faith sings. Martin Luther does not mince words about this:

> There is now in the New Testament a better service of God, of which the Psalm [96:1] here says: 'Sing to the Lord a new song. Sing to the Lord all the earth.' For

God has cheered our hearts and minds through his dear Son, whom he gave for us to redeem us from sin, death, and the devil. He who believes this earnestly cannot be quiet about it. But he must gladly and willingly sing and speak about it.[5]

When one fully comes to grips with the redemption that we have received from Jesus Christ, our faith cannot help but erupt in song. Not in a cheesy, contrived, Broadway manner, but in a way that is genuinely heartfelt and that seeks to give honor to God and proclaim all that God has done for us through His Son. Consider just a few well-known events from Scripture where faith boils over into singing.

After the Israelites had been led safely across the Red Sea and freed from the Egyptians, they feared the Lord, believed His promises, and responded by singing a hymn (Exodus 15:1–18; ESV); the first two verses are "I will sing to the Lord, for he has triumphed gloriously; the horse and his rider he has thrown into the sea. The Lord is my strength and my song, and he has become my salvation; this is my God, and I will praise him, my father's God, and I will exalt him."

Mary, when visiting Elizabeth and being recognized as the woman who had been blessed to give birth to the son of God, proclaimed God's goodness to all generations in her great hymn (Luke 1:46–55) that begins, "My soul magnifies the Lord, and my spirit rejoices in God my Savior." At the birth of Christ, the multitude of the heavenly host sang, "Glory to God in the highest, and on earth peace among those with whom he is pleased!" (Luke 2:14). And Simeon, after personally being in the presence of the child Jesus, the Christ, sang his hymn (Luke 2:29–32), beginning "Lord, now you are letting your servant depart in peace, according to your word."

We don't sing in the divine liturgy of the Church to kill time or to help get ourselves into the right mood. We don't sing to entertain ourselves by singing only our favorite hymns. We sing because the Church sings, because faith sings. By the grace of the Holy Spirit we have been granted faith and so we sing to recount and proclaim that faith.

The reason the Church sings this faith is because God has first sung to us. "The Lord your God is in your midst, a mighty one who will save; he will rejoice over you with gladness; he will quiet you by his love; he will exult over you with loud singing" (Zephaniah 3:17). This is what clearly distinguishes a church musician from a musician who happens to work in the church. The church musician recognizes that the source of the song is God and that the subject of the song is Christ. The church musician teaches that this song is all at once a song of celebration, a song of love, a song of peace, a song of sorrow, and a song of victory. It is the eternal song: the song that knows no stylistic boundaries. It is the song of all creation. It is the song of life eternal. It is the song that allows us to sing with boldness and confidence, "I know that my Redeemer lives, and that at the last he will stand upon the earth. And after my skin has been thus destroyed, yet in my flesh I shall see God" (Job 19:25–26).

"It Shall Be Told of the Lord to the Coming Generation"

The church musician teaches us about Christ through our singing. Our singing is not an end unto itself but rather it is a means to an end. Singing psalms, hymns, and spiritual songs is one way of continuing to be in the Word, one way of growing more mature in our faith, and one way of "teaching and admonishing one another in all wisdom" (Colossians 3:16).

St. Paul clearly connects the act of singing with the act of teaching. When texts that convey Biblical truths are set to music, and the words, pitches, and rhythms are uttered from our lips, the content is placed into our hearts. The hymns and psalms that we sing stay with us throughout our lives and remain with us as we reach our final hours. These notes help the texts live within us. They are stored in the closets of our minds, and when we need them most we are able to draw upon them and use them to remind us of God's grace and mercy, to help us to pray, and to strengthen our faith.

Article XV of the Apology of the Augsburg Confession (XV 40) states that "the children chant the Psalms in order to learn them; the people also sing in order either to learn or to pray."[6]

Our singing throughout our lifetime teaches us lessons about Christ and about our faith that we draw upon when we need them most. When keeping vigil by a loved one in their final hours, these songs give voice to our prayer: "Teach me to live that I may dread / The grave as little as my bed. / Teach me to die that so I may / Rise glorious at the awe-full day."[7] When the powers of death have done their worst and we stand at the graveside hearing the words "ashes to ashes, dust to dust," our song has taught us to sing, "The strife is o'er, the battle done; / Now is the victor's triumph won."[8] When we are caught amid the many tangles and snares that Satan throws our way, our song teaches us that "Though the road ahead be thorny, / Though dark clouds all light obscure, / Though my cross-shaped path grows steeper, / With the Lord, I am secure."[9]And, through it all, we gladly and willingly sing, "I am baptized into Christ; / I'm a child of paradise!"[10]

Singing together is a method of encouragement. People sing for all sorts of various reasons, but the act of singing together reminds us that we are not alone on this journey, that we share common joys and sorrows. We have been given to each other as brothers and sisters in Christ, and so we rejoice with those who rejoice and mourn with those who mourn. This, really, is the essence of human community.

Before our Father's throne
We pour our ardent prayers;
Our fears, our hopes, our aims are one,
Our comforts and our cares."[11]

"Christ Be My Teacher in Age as in Youth"

It's sometimes difficult to explain this in our culture today, but musicians are not the same as iPods, and live music is not the same as recorded music. You can download your favorite performance of any particular piece and listen to it over and over and it will always sound the same. But before any piece is recorded and downloaded, one or more musicians make many decisions about how they will perform the song or piece. Musicians do not simply look at dots on a page, hit the mental "play" button, and magically create well-crafted music. Those decisions revolve around the art of interpretation, and this is terribly important because sound is not neutral: it carries meaning. In the Church, a good interpretation can teach—just as the text of a hymn can teach—because it can draw us into the text by creating certain sound images in our mind. This is what Aaron Copland referred to as the "sonorous image," which, he said, plays a critical role in the meaning of any piece of music.

Shortly after joining the faculty of Concordia College (now Concordia University) in Ann Arbor, MI, in the fall of 1992, I was excited to learn that Charles Ore was coming to nearby Livonia to play a hymn festival celebrating the dedication of a new Casavant organ at Christ Our Savior Lutheran Church. The festival began with "Prepare the Royal Highway," and Charles used his setting found in *11 Compositions for Organ*, set 5,[12] to introduce the hymn. His use of the double pedal and parallel fifths (which, by the way, I thought you were never supposed to play on the organ), created a clear and vivid picture in my imagination of the procession on the royal highway. The sharp, crisp, fanfare rhythms and bright, brilliant registrations vividly portrayed the call to "greet the King of Glory / Foretold in sacred story," as this hymn states.[13] I even remember my heart pounding so much that I wanted to "shout and sing!" (But being a good Lutheran, I decided just to sing and not to stand up and shout.)

Charles taught me again that day. As a congregation member that evening, I was reminded of the nature of the coming King through Charles' composition and his playing. As a fellow church musician and organist, I was reminded once again of the importance of interpretation, just as Charles had done a few years earlier through his previous collection of pieces.

I met Charles for the first time that evening after the hymn festival. I introduced myself to him, asked if that piece in particular was published, and complimented him on his interpretations, which I found to be unique and exciting. He, of course, responded with his characteristic grin and a humble "thank you." Through his response, he reminded me that the music was not about him, it was about Christ. (The next morning, I had to order set 5, by the way.)

Onward in Peace[14]

In the summer of 2002 I was both humbled and honored to be appointed professor of music and university organist at Concordia University Nebraska in Seward. I was to be Charles Ore's successor following his retirement after he had held this position for nearly 35 years. I was a bit anxious as I prepared to make the journey westward to the great plains of Nebraska. Not only did I have the task of filling Charles' position, I would also be working with him, as Charles intended to keep teaching organ at Concordia on a part-time basis.

Working side by side with Charles from 2002 until 2015 was a true pleasure. His warm and welcoming personality, his enthusiasm for the organ and for quality church music, his strong desire to be a creative musician, and his love for our students was infectious. Through our many conversations in the Music Center, Charles continued to teach me, not in a forceful way, but in an encouraging one. His comments were not designed to turn me into a clone of him but rather were aimed at helping me grow as a musician, as an organist, and as a teacher. Through these conversations, he not only encouraged me, he helped to train the next generation of musicians, those who will carry the song of the Church forward.

The church musician helps to ensure the continuation of the song of the Church by teaching the next generation of musicians about what it means to be a musician, how to be a better musician, how to be a leader, and how to use one's gifts in service to the Church.

In the congregation, this involves teaching the children in a very intentional manner. If children develop a love for and appreciation of the song of the Church at an early age, it will likely stick with them and continue to grow throughout their lifetime. As the Psalmist prays, "it shall be told of the Lord to the coming generation; they shall come and proclaim his righteousness to a people yet unborn" (Ps. 22:30–31). The majority of those children will most likely not become professional musicians but rather will be music lovers and active music-makers in the church. There are some, however, who will indeed become professional musicians. and perhaps some will choose to serve the Church with their music because of their church musician's example and encouragement. I know that is the case for both my wife and me, and I suspect the same is true for many of us in the field.

The church musician is called to teach in so many different ways. Charles Ore's career exemplifies this so well, as he has taught many, many people over the years through his work at the university, through his playing, conducting, leading, and composing. And so, as we give thanks for the work of Charles Ore, we also pray that the Lord of the Church would continue to

> Take my hands and let them move
> At the impulse of thy love;
> Take my feet and let them be
> Swift and beautiful for thee.
>
> Take my voice and let me sing
> Always, only for my King;
> Take my lips and let them be
> Filled with messages from thee.[15]

Notes

1 Ore's syllabus for organ study at Concordia in Seward, NE, always began with this statement.

2 *The Book of Concord: The Confessions of the Evangelical Lutheran Church* [BC], ed. by Robert Kolb and Timothy J. Wengert (Minneapolis: Fortress Press, 2000), 229.

3 Dietrich Bonhoeffer, *Life Together* (New York: Harper & Row, 1954), 66–68.

4 LSB, p. 250.

5 Martin Luther, *Luther's Works*, American edition, vol. 53, *Liturgy and Hymns*, ed. Ulrich S. Leupold (Philadelphia: Fortress, 1965), 333.

6 BC, 229.

7 The Commission on Worship of The Lutheran Church—Missouri Synod, *Lutheran Service Book* [LSB] (St. Louis: Concordia, 2006), 883, st. 3.

8 LSB 464, st. 1.

9 LSB 753, st. 5.

10 LSB 594, st. 5.

11 LSB 649, st. 2.

12 Charles W. Ore, 11 *Compositions for Organ*, set 5 (St. Louis: Concordia, 1991).

13 LSB 343, st. 1.

14 Ore's e-mail signature closed with this statement.

15 LSB 783, 784, sts. 3 and 4.

Hymns and the Care of the Soul

REFLECTIONS BY CONNIE ORE†,
WITH COMMENTARY BY IRENE BEETHE

Lord, let at last Thine angels come,
To Abr'ham's bosom bear me home,
That I may die unfearing;
And in its narrow chamber keep
My body safe in peaceful sleep
Until thy reappearing.
And then from death awaken me,
That these mine eyes with joy may see,
O Son of God, Thy glorious face,
My Savior and my fount of grace.
Lord Jesus Christ, my prayer attend, my prayer attend,
And I will praise Thee without end.[1]

This hymn is often said or sung at the bedside of dying Christians, giving comfort and hope to them as they near the end of life. Throughout the life of the Church, hymns are used to proclaim the Gospel and to provide a voice in times of joy and sorrow, of life and death, when our own words fail. The church musician's role is to guide the singing of these hymns in such a way that faith is deepened and its truths etched into the soul.

As a musician of the church, Charles Ore accepted this responsibility seriously, and his example encourages those of us who seek to do likewise. Yet he did not do so alone. In addition to his myriad brother and sister musicians within the Church, he had one particular partner who sustained him, body, mind, and soul: his wife, Connie. She, too, assumed the task of church musician with a spirit of commitment and joy that demonstrates to this day how the church's music nourishes the people of God not only in their living but also in their dying.

The congregations they served were blessed with the skill and care with which they led hymnody. Introductions, hymn concertatos, or descants were carefully chosen or written with the text in mind. How would the music be an effective messenger of the Gospel? They shared ideas and wrote compositions together. If Charles wrote a composition, he valued Connie's opinion. She was his toughest critic! She provided not only a musical ear but a unique perspective about Charles and his writing. They were servants of the Church, helping instill the faith into the lives of God's people.

In December 2005 Connie fell ill, and on January 20, 2006, Charles and Connie were told the diagnosis of the illness that had come to live inside her body: myelodysplastic syndrome (MDS). The hymns that had given comfort to others would now strengthen and console her as she struggled against the disease that would ultimately end her life in September 2010. Faith, etched in her soul in part by hymnody, would be tested and tried. In her first blog posting, titled "My New Life, January 2006," she wrote, "Charles and I thank you for your prayers, and your caring and your concern—you have called and sent flowers and cards and you have wrapped us round with such cherishing! We remain optimistic and hopeful for good outcomes, always remembering that we are in God's love and care."[2] This hope is expressed beautifully in the prayer they prayed together often: "Lord God, You have called Your servants to ventures of which we cannot see the ending, by paths as yet untrodden, through perils unknown. Give us faith to go out with good courage, not knowing where we go, but only that Your hand is leading us and Your love supporting us; through Jesus Christ our Lord."[3]

Connie's gift for writing allowed people from across the country—and perhaps the world—to experience hymns in a new way as she wrote about her disease in her blog. In those five years she often would quote hymn texts and express her faith by relating them to her "new life" with MDS. What follows are excerpts from entries in her blog, instances where hymns carried her through the last part of her life to her "new life" with Jesus. You may read entire entries at http://www.constanceore.com. (Endnotes have been added.)

* * *

March 28, 2006

After being given a reprieve from treatment for a bit, Connie went for a walk with her dog, Alphie, in the Sanctuary, the land around their home.

The antidote comes with melody and words—all the years of playing hymns and reading texts have left a gathering of fragments of verses and tunes. Today's words speak from "There in God's Garden."

> There in God's garden stands the Tree of Wisdom, . . .
> See how its branches reach to us in welcome;
> Hear what the Voice says, "Come to me, ye weary!
> Give me your sickness, give me all your sorrow,
> I will give blessing."[4]

A hymn writer's words from so long ago reach across time to carry me forward into another day, and for this too I am thankful.

July 31, 2006

Connie was asked to write an essay on the subject of "Music and Suffering" for a quarterly publication called Suffering. *It was published by Stauros U.S.A., a nonprofit organization founded by the Congregation of the Passion in 1973. The organization and publication are no longer in existence. Here is her essay.*

Music and Suffering—A Singular Perspective

Both the words "music" and "suffering" embrace definitions, thoughts, ideas, and nuances large enough to have given birth to thousands of books, lectures, pieces of art, films, sermons, and concerts. There has been an endless array of attempts made by the wise and thoughtful to elucidate these subjects that touch every human experience. How can one person with one experience add to this? This question, particularly when focused on myself, seems foolish when held to the comparative narratives of greatness—both in musical perception and in suffering. Only when it can be placed as a small piece in the mosaic of understanding can such an undertaking be logically pursued.

"I've been asked to write about 'Music and Suffering,'" I said to my husband. "What do you think about that?" "I certainly can relate to that," he replied fervently. "I know I've suffered through a lot of music in my day." That made me smile, but I quickly clarified. "That is missing the point entirely," I said, and proceeded to explain more fully the concept as I understood it, and he conceded that yes, he had shot wide. I did not need to point out to him that he too has joined my new life's experience with an incurable disease in a most immediate way. Sickness of the blood is so very intimate. You can't wad up the evil thing into a tumor or lump or breast or kidney or eye. Blood is essential, and mine seems hopelessly flawed. When the white cells diminished and diminished, this blood not only didn't stop infections, it began to invite microbes and invaders to flourish. By itself the blood disease doesn't cause pain or prickles, but it carries fear throughout the system. Fear of clotting—here today, tomorrow a vegetable, everybody's nightmare—as close as the next heartbeat. Fear of infections, scratch, red streaks away, fear. The pastor shook my hand yesterday in his finest greeting and I couldn't wait to wash it with disinfectant.

The year is 1949, and it is a spring morning in the confirmation room of a white-painted rural Lutheran school on an Iowa hill. The pastor is teaching a lesson on "suffering," which is never to be forgotten. This man has dark eyes and a thin moustache, and the very black hair on his head is combed straight back from a widow's peak. He has arrived at our out-of-the-way rural parish because of a mysterious nervous breakdown having something to do with his chaplaincy in the Second World War. He is very intense and he has placed a crucifix on the table before us. Then he says something like this: "Our Lord Jesus Christ suffered and died for our sins. He was literally nailed up and hung there." Our eyes are fixed upon the crucifix, which had the crown of thorns and the spikes in the hands and feet. The pastor looks at the five of us in that year's confirmation class, and inquires, "Now, what does that mean to you, he suffered and died for your sins?" His voice is challenging, and we know that our answers had better be good. I still remember thinking that I hadn't done anything that could possibly bring on such agony. "Your sins" he says again, implacably. I ventured that maybe what we did added up, like not obeying our parents or really, really wanting to hurt one of our brothers, and he said with approval, yes, exactly, and not only that, but every single sin that we would commit throughout our life, and every single sin that every single human would commit throughout their lives was punished right there on that cross. That was suffering, he told us, that was really suffering. We all sat and looked at the crucifix for what seemed like a long time. I believe I carried this measuring stick through the years, never applying the word or concept to any of my own life experiences. When contemplating this writing project, I asked a group of friends how they defined suffering. One said something like this: "Suffering is anything that carries you outside the place of your perception of well-being. It can range from uneasiness about something through the worst kind of agony." This seems a good and complete definition with which to work. After thinking that I knew a lot more about music than suffering, within the week, I experienced an arterial blood clot in the kidney, which killed a third of the living tissue there because of a lack of blood. In this experience, there was and still is a great deal of physical pain. It was as though, the moment I needed it, I was provided with a teeth-clenching, hair-pulling example of physical suffering, with a degree of mental anguish added in that the doctors said they had not seen anything like this before when dealing with my type of cancer, and therefore the possibility of it happening again, randomly and unexpectedly, became an added concern.

That music works as a palliative to suffering is well known. How and to what degree this happens is totally subjective, so discourse about it must also be addressed subjectively. In this essay, I will explain how it is for me. The musical element of "melody" is defined as a series of tones that move forward in one of three ways: by repetition, by going upward in pitch by steps or leaps, or by going downward by steps or leaps. When I taught music to seventh graders, I would play a game with them to demonstrate that each of us carries a large number of melodies within. For example, I would play "Name the Tune" and say, "Christmas song," then sound the first two tones of the carol, "Joy to the World." Since all of us came from a like cultural tradition, one half or more of the children would guess the song on as little as two opening pitches. In this way I would show the class the miracle of a collection of large numbers of melodies in each of our heads, just waiting to be recalled. As years pass, melodies gather, stored behind doors of which we often are unaware. Then a certain scent, a south wind, a friend's laugh—any unexpected thing can fling open that door and the song is there, waiting. It is waiting to come and help heal during times of suffering as well.

A lifetime of playing hymns and teaching songs has provided me with a sizable collection from which to choose, and this music is as near as the next thought. When pain's suffering is my human experience, there are songs bearing the poetry of psalmists and hymn writers to give me comfort. The miracle of music is that it can illuminate a deity as nothing else can. God is experienced by all of humankind, in some fashion, but God is experienced by each of us, one at a time, and uniquely so. Music is the same: its sounds are everywhere, impossible not to hear, but yet experienced by each of us, one pair of ears at a time and uniquely so.

Walking into the forest on a sunlit spring morning wondering why the disease has become the predominant shape and color of my day, I look upward to see two red tail hawks floating on the wind, apparently just for the fun of it, and the song, "Come away to the skies, my beloved, arise and rejoice in the day you were born" sings loud and joyful. The creator God is near; the shapes and sounds of the natural world force the thoughts away from myself, reminding me that I am just a small gathering of tissues moving through a huge sphere.

When I was a director of music, I planned worship services and became very adept at timing hymns' length, so I have a time clock already in place for a stanza of hymnody; for example, one verse of "In Thee Is Gladness" lasts approximately 50 seconds, so I know that singing it through will take me past 50 seconds of present pain. The words will help me: "He sees and blesses / In worst distresses, / He can change them with a breath."[5] Perhaps I will sing it again and again, and so the journey through the valley moves forward. The doctor says, "This will hurt, but it'll be over in 20 seconds." I sing out loud so I can't hear the sounds of the intrusion. "Have no fear, little flock; / Have no fear, little flock, / For the Father has chosen / To give you the Kingdom; / Have no fear, little flock."[6] (Time: 18 seconds) "Do I need another verse?" I ask. "No, we're done." he says, and I am thankful. "Thankful hearts raise to God; / Thankful hearts raise to God, / For He stays close beside you, / In all things works with you; / Thankful hearts raise to God."[7] This time I am silent outside, but inside, the organ is full and children's voices are loud and true.

There is music created during times of suffering, and when it is sent out into the world, it is there to aid and comfort the listener. Here is a story excerpted from a Minnesota Public Radio interview with Paul and Ruth Manz. One of the Manz's children, their three-year-old son John, came down with a childhood illness that threatened to end his life. "And at one point he was given up by the doctor as well as the staff," Paul says. Paul and Ruth Manz took turns at their son's bedside: Ruth by day, Paul by night. Ruth is a gifted lyricist and always on the lookout for ways to inspire her husband's composing. "I'm the underling. She calls the shots," Paul says, "In this particular case she was the spark plug . . . the spark plug that suggested the text," he says.

During their vigil Ruth brought Paul some words she'd crafted based on a text in Revelation. "Peace be to you and grace from Him who freed us from our sins. Who loved us all and shed his blood that we might saved be. Sing holy, holy to our Lord, the Lord almighty God, who was and is and is to come, sing holy, holy Lord," Ruth says. "That is just a compilation of the theme in Revelation, Revelation 22, where it speaks of the longing of the Advent, actually, the coming of the Christ," she adds. "I think we'd reached the point where we felt that time was certainly running out so we committed it to the Lord and said, 'Lord Jesus quickly come,'" Ruth says. "I made a sketch that night at the bedside and miraculously through prayer by a lot of people John survived," Paul says. That's the story of the hymn "E'en So, Lord Jesus, Quickly Come." Ruth and Paul Manz's son John is [now] in his 50s and has the original score of the hymn written while he was ill.

This is an example of music born of suffering that brings joy to all who sing and hear it. This song has become popular not only throughout this country but also in other countries. There are countless musical compositions that have had their beginnings in such times that then await the needing listener's ear.

Perhaps there are times and places in suffering where there is no song. A hymn writer paraphrases Psalm 137: "By the Babylonian rivers we sat down in grief and wept; hung our harps upon a willow, mourned for Zion when we slept." I have always been struck by the finality of the image of hanging the harps in the willow trees by the river before crossing to the other side. No songs to take along into exile; in suffering, perhaps there are times when no song can be heard because we have been taken to the other side where the music is silent. I have not been there in my journey but the shadow of that possibility has been felt around the corners of my life experience. I walk and cry in the forest, and there is no music to be heard, for my fear is of the unknown. Death is waiting for all of us, but for me it has an immediacy that did not exist prior to my disease. All of the knowledge I have of love and peace, sensation and security, cherishing and being cherished, sheer joy and gaiety exists in the now, in this sphere. Great and generous gifts of God these have been, and though I want desperately to have the total trust that is so often spoken of in discourses on faith and God's goodness toward us in all things, it is not yet complete, so I cry and I am still afraid and when that happens there is no music to be heard. Blessedly, the new day comes, the new sunrise brings light, and the songs begin again because hope is irrepressible. "'Hope' is the thing with feathers / That perches in the soul / And sings the tune without the words / And never stops at all."[8]

Music is one of the conduits to the sacred sphere. When I am trapped within the body which is in the throes of pain or loss or change, sometimes the only way to endure, or to "pass through the valley of the shadow of death," is through the sounds of music. At such times one wants to plead with God first for surcease; if that is not possible, then for mercy, for strength, or just endurance. When the thoughts are too plain and too near to help, it is a fine thing to recall a poet's expressions carried on a composer's melody. The music pulls God nearer to you; faith and trust in assistance from a greater power than your own can propel you forward into a place of survival. When we suffer, music can come to meet us and help us. It can come from within the great storehouse of songs that many of us hold inside, or from history, or from newly composed works. It may come in the form of a psalm, where the very words sing, or in the melody of a musical written for Broadway. It may be instrumental, it may be tonal or atonal, it may be voices carrying wonderful texts, or simply voices carrying melodies. Suffering is and will be a part of life, but at such times, music can strengthen and lift the heart. It can open perceptions of  a God who is in every place—within, without, near as breath, yet vast as the universe. This is a gift of the Creator to humankind that can help and heal until such time when one joins in the making of the beautiful and perfect music that is sounding in God's heavenly Kingdom, now and forevermore.

December 29, 2006

Connie reflects on the music of Christmas 2006.

This Christmas I can't remember much of the music at all. I think that the familiar carols have been so wrung out, minced, diced, trimmed, and manipulated in hopes of something new sounding forth that the brain pushes the mute button without voluntary thought. Even the boys' choir in the traditional English Lessons and Carols began to sound a bit shrill as they sang ever-higher descants over newly composed materials that combined atonality with Latin texts and complex harmonies. The best musical experience came at the evening service with Charles playing and the congregation  singing the familiar songs with great delight. When our family gathers tomorrow, we will sing the carols together and bring them home to the heart again.

September 13, 2007

Blood counts are a part of her new life, and even when the numbers weren't as good as previously recorded, a hymn would reflect the day.

On Tuesday, the reading was at 2.2, going down from the previous week's 3.3. I still feel quite good, with energy to enjoy life and nature's nuances in this small quiet place in the universe. There are many hymns that live in my mind that put words to the emotion and make me smile as their words spin past: for example, to the tune Lasst uns erfreuen (a melody that has verses and verses of happy thanksgiving), I can hear:

> To you, O God, all creatures sing,
> and all creation, everything,
> sings your praises, alleluia! . . .
>
> Your wind that blows the tempest by,
> your clouds that sail across the sky,
> sing your praises, alleluia!
> Your morning rises with a song,
> and lights of evening sing along,
> sing your praises, alleluia,
> alleluia, alleluia, alleluia! [9]

November 16, 2007

I am better now, and I know that as before, there were many praying people pushing and pulling me out of the dark places of pain and unknowable outcomes. I kept thinking of the hymn verse from "Earth and All Stars" where the hymn writer says, "Daughter and son, / Loud praying members, / sing to the Lord a new song. / . . . he has done marvelous things, / I too will praise him  with a new song!" [10] It's the "loud praying members" that I heard through congregations and cards and spoken words of encouragement.

December 20, 2007

Christmas now, in just five days! The past weeks have centered on cookies, cards. and gifts, and those have taken up all energy and time. In the "olden" days, there were also parties, Christmas music preparations, and endless children's program rehearsals, and my present self views that in awe. Charles says very matter-of-fact-ly, "That was then, this is now." We have had snow and glittering

trees for days, actually living in the Christmas-card settings that often arrive in the form of Christmas-card illustrations. Fortunately, we do not have to harness horses and travel by sleigh as frequent-ly depicted, though my mother's stories of going to Hanover [township] church in a horse-drawn cutter, wrapped in fur robes and through the snow-covered land on a moonlit night, still fills the  heart with nostalgia. She would tell of the bells on the horses sound-ing from every direction as families came to the church.

My childhood memories of the Christmas Eve event are cen-tered on the same landscape and in the same church in the country. Perhaps the brightest picture is one in which I solo for the second verse of "O Little Town of Bethlehem": "For Christ is born of Mary, / and gathered all above." I was in the second grade and stood in the middle of the front of the church, and I was wearing a dress with a red velveteen top and a satin plaid skirt. As I sang, I still see the faces looking at me with ever-growing smiles upon them. I was very pleased because I assumed it was delight in my singing; unfor-tunately, it apparently was that I was twisting my skirt in my hand, which was getting shorter and shorter, and the smiles were about whether my modesty would be compromised before the end of the verse. Never sure of the outcome, this may well have been the end of a budding operatic career.

In earlier times, my persona would be described as "delicate" or perhaps even "frail," though my physical appearance is neither. My immunities are edgy, aches seem to compound, and my en-ergy feels as though it is receding somewhat. This is not yet worth complaining about, since all is better than what might have been. Charles' father would always reply to con-cerns about his health by saying, "Not bad,  and it's better than the alternative," so that phrase has been added to the commentary in the family. My blood readings indicated that they held their own, with just a small drop in the red counts. The next reading takes place the day after Christmas. So I delight in and savor these days—as I lie awake in the early morning hours, there are Christmas celebrations from past years playing through my mind, and carols and songs sing on and on in my head. Upon occasion this means that my first words of the morning to Charles might be, "How does the third verse of 'Joy to the World' begin?" There will be grand music in the next days, and the wonderful and familiar story of Jesus' birth will be told in word and song.

March 3, 2008

This new month is filled with promise: political voices calling for "change," spring concerts, a daughter's birthday, Palm Sunday, and Easter. Yesterday, I could sing! One of the sorry things of the last two years has been the loss of my singing voice—the only place where it all sounded fine was inside of my head; the actual vocal production was abysmal. Then yesterday, in the singing of the hymns, my voice was present and true and it was an incredible delight. The woman sitting in front of me complimented me, and it took a measure of self-control to simply thank her instead of clasping her to my bosom and telling her the entire story of my life.

The last hymn was "What Wondrous Love Is This," and its final verses were especially well-suited to my day.

> To God and to the Lamb I will sing, I will sing;
> To God and to the Lamb I will sing;
> To God and to the Lamb, Who is the great I Am,
> While millions join the theme, I will sing, I will sing.
> While millions join the theme, I will sing.
>
> And when from death I'm free, I'll sing on, I'll sing on;
> And when from death I'm free, I'll sing on.
> And when from death I'm free, I'll sing his love for me,
> And through eternity I'll sing on, I'll sing on;
> And through eternity I'll sing on.[11]

March 18, 2008

Children bearing palms ushered in Holy Week on Sunday, beginning a time of remembering the central teachings and beliefs of the Christian church concerning Christ's redemptive sacrifice for humanity. Maundy Thursday's commemoration of Christ's last supper, Good Friday's somber remembrance of Christ's crucifixion, and Easter's grand celebration of his triumph over death as dawn light reveals an empty tomb are celebrated around the world. This has gone on for centuries as the faithful  remember anew the miracle that connects earthly existence with eternal life. We will be a part of it, too: Charles will play the music and I will stand with the congregation. On Easter morning we will say with delight, "Christ is risen!" and "He is risen indeed!"

April 29, 2008

Up through endless ranks of angels,
Cries of triumph in His ears,
To His heav'nly throne ascending,
Having vanquished all their fears,
Christ looks down upon His faithful,
Leaving them in happy tears."[12]

So states the first verse of an Ascension hymn written to pitches that move swiftly upward, and the imagery of "endless ranks of angels" surely appears like those wonderful cumulous clouds stacked into thunderheads that we see in our summer skies. The Church celebrates Christ's ascension from earth to heaven on May 1st this year, and Christendom joyfully lives on with the mystery of God's presence still here, yet there in heaven and in all places in between.

July 15, 2008

In the summer hymn sings that Charles has presided over these last weeks, the hymn "Abide with Me" has been requested nearly every Sunday, and it carries me back to the little church of my parents and the occasions of their funerals. It was a favorite of both of them, and we sang it there as we gathered to honor them one more time. Now, when I hear the familiar words and sing the familiar melody, I am carried both back and forward in time as memories and comfort intertwine in a wonderful way.

Abide with me, fast falls the eventide
The darkness deepens; Lord with me abide.
When other helpers fail and comforts flee
Help of the helpless, O abide with me.

Swift to its close ebbs out life's little day;
Earth's joys grow dim, its glories pass away;
Change and decay in all around I see;
O thou who changest not, abide with me.

Hold Thou Thy cross before my closing eyes;
Shine through the gloom, and point me to the skies.
Heav'n's morning breaks, and earth's vain shadows flee;
In life, in death, O Lord, abide with me.[13]

August 19, 2008

My energy has begun to sag in recent days; moving my body through space feels as though the molecules around me are heavy and there is no lightness in my being. "Up, get up!" instructs the mind, and the physical self reluctant-ly moves. We meet with the oncologist on Friday of this week. How life proceeds is much on my mind— hopefully information and wisdom will meet and the direction will be clear. It seems that there are two  options available—more chemotherapy or let life go on to its con-clusion without attempting another intervention.

God who made the earth and heaven,
Darkness and light:
You the day for work have given,
For rest the night.
May Your angel guards defend us,
Slumber sweet Your mercy send us,
Holy dreams and hopes attend us
All through the night.

And when morn again shall call us
To run life's way,
May we still, what-e'er befall us,
Your will obey. . . .

Guard us waking, guard us sleeping,
And when we die,
May we in Your mighty keeping
All peaceful lie.[14]

September 2, 2008

For me, faith needs to be considered and regarded daily. It seems to change shape and form constantly because it encompasses so much that is unseen. There are the hints and reminders of a creating and sustaining God that one finds in nature: the sight of newly designed sunrises and ever-changing cloud forms, the sounds of season-changing winds and supportive rains falling, and always—right overhead—the mystery of the stars and the universe. There are the touches of angels in the smiles and words of dear ones around a person, in the thoughtfulness of friends and nurses and doctors and good people. How this is perceived is held inside of each person's own mind, and here it is that the conversation with God is heard. I think it is easy to understand "pray without ceasing" because God is so present.

This last week has been one in which I have thought about living in faith a great deal. My visit to my primary care doctor ended with a friendly admonition to take care, wash hands, avoid children, school settings, and church, because they would be the most dangerous places to pick up infections for which I have no defenses. I left knowing that two dear granddaughters would be arriving for a stay of several days, and that my weekly worship experience would need to continue—Charles always has new and wonderful music that wraps the hymn texts and readings in beautiful sound colors, and I go forward refreshed. But then I frequently get sick for a day or more, and my circle of life is pulled "out of round." It was that way last weekend, too, but my contemplations of living in faith lead me to think that life has to be lived and I must not fear the outcomes.

November 5, 2008

Throughout these times, as I walk through field and forest and consider ultimate verities, I find that it is always the words and sounds of the spiritual songs and hymns that comfort me most. Usually, I have only fragments of the words, so when I get back, I will find them and sing them beautifully and loudly, all within my head where my voice resembles Renée Fleming at her finest. Here is the first verse of this day's walk.

> Thy holy wings, O Savior, spread gently over me,
> and let me rest securely through good and ill in thee.
> Oh, be my strength and portion, my rock and hiding place,
> and let my ev'ry moment be lived within thy grace.[15]

December 2, 2008

Advent has come with its beautiful music and myriad preparations. Since these songs haven't joined the sound assault of endless commercial renditions of the once-beloved Christmas carols, the Advent hymns can still present lovely words and melodies without having to pass through the loudspeakers and torturous tinsel tones of mall music. Charles played his setting of "Come, O Long-Expected Jesus" on Sunday, and it was a wonderful beginning to a wonderful season.

> Come, O long-expected Jesus, born to set your people free;
> from our fears and sins release us by your death on Calvary.
> Israel's strength and consolation,
>   hope to all the earth impart,
> Dear desire of every nation, joy of every longing heart.
>
> Born your people to deliver, born a child and yet a king.
> Born to reign in us forever,
>   now your gracious kingdom bring.
> By your own eternal Spirit rule in all our hearts alone;
> By your all-sufficient merit raise us to your glorious throne.[16]

March 24, 2009

The hymn that I am trying to memorize this week is "Come Away to the Skies," a Charles Wesley text set to music found in "A Supplement to the Kentucky Harmony" (the tune is MIDDLEBURY). The words seem very compelling to me at this time.

Come away to the skies, my beloved, arise
and rejoice in the day you were born;
On this festival day, come exulting away,
And with singing to Zion return.

For thy glory we were first created to share
both the nature and kingdom divine;
now created again, that our lives may remain
throughout time and eternity thine.

We with thanks do approve the design of that love
which has joined us to Jesus' name;
so united in heart, let us nevermore part,
till we meet at the feast of the Lamb.[17]

May 12, 2009

As life goes forward, I hear in my mind Charles playing his composition, "What a Friend We Have in Jesus," and I replay the words
that I loved to sing loudly (complete with the sliding tone between
"Je" and "sus") when I was about eight years old. I hear his exu-
berant and energetic presentation of that old well-worn hymn and I
think, "Oh yes."

What a friend we have in Jesus,
All our sins and griefs to bear!
What a privilege to carry
Everything to God in prayer!
Oh, what peace we often forfeit;
Oh, what needless pain we bear—
All because we do not carry
Everything to God in prayer![18]

August 25, 2009

School's beginning signals summer's end. This summer of 2009
is going to be placed into our record books by the wonderful organ
composition created by Charles Ore, the composer. He began with
the unlikely hymn "Rock of Ages." I think the phrase "When I soar
to worlds unknown" called to him because we had been in discussion
about what happens after death, and this imagery evokes wonderful

things. The poetry is attributed to Augustus Toplady who lived in the 1700s, and the hymn also contains enough obtuse and tortured imagery that many of the pastors I worked with avoided using the hymn entirely. (I.e. "Foul, I to the fountain fly"—I always thought perhaps it should have read "Fowl," considering the flying part.)

Charles has named his piece "Glory Rock" and divided it into five parts. The first, called "Rock," uses the familiar melody but placed into a classic rock format. The second movement is titled "Could My Zeal No Respite Know," from the hymn text, but here presented with an ironic touch. Then comes "The Double" ("Be of sin the double cure" is the poetry—the movement dances between melody and echo patterns). At the beginning of the fourth movement the piece adds melodic material from "The Battle Hymn of the Republic": "Mine eyes have seen the glory of the coming of the Lord" and this part is called "The Coming." The composition concludes with "When I Soar to Worlds Unknown" and this is the most extraordinary part of all. Here Charles uses a double pedal, right foot outlining "Rock of Ages" and left foot playing "Glory, glory, hallelujah," while the hands are doing incredible fast patterns in the manner of French toccata material and reminiscent of Arthur Honegger's symphonic poem *Pacific 231*. After he developed the piece, Charles invited me to come and hear him play it on the new organ that fills the front of the recital hall at Concordia. Since then, I have repeatedly asked him to play it for me because it is such a splendid experience. As I watch the Casavant making the music, I can see it responding to the man at the console. When the piece begins with powerful, large, low and strong chords, the organ plants its feet solidly and says, "I can do *rock*." In the second movement, where the sounds are playful, it almost seems to smile, and then as the piece builds and builds, it truly seems to become one with the player. As the echo of the huge final chord dies away, the organ seems to settle back in contentment saying, "My, that was fun!"

September 8, 2009

We always have hope and the comfort of faith that includes acceptance of what life contains. Therefore the prayers go on: *"Guide us waking, O Lord, and guard us sleeping that awake we may watch with Christ and asleep we may rest in peace,*[19] and the spiritual songs continue to sound. In the hymn "The Day Thou Gavest" the poet says

> The day Thou gavest, Lord, is ended,
> The darkness falls at Thy behest;
> To Thee our morning hymns ascended,
> Thy praise shall sanctify our rest.
>
> As o'er each continent and island
> The dawn leads on another day.
> The voice of prayer is never silent,
> Nor dies the strain of praise away.
>
> The sun, that bids us rest, is waking
> Thy saints beneath the western skies,
> And hour by hour, as day is breaking,
> Fresh hymns of thankful praise arise.[20]

These are small examples of the many that accompany me on my journey.

September 22, 2009

While we have always lived by faith, these present days and those ahead seem to require a greater measure of trust in God's mercy, since a weakening of the body requires a strengthening of resources in other places. In the Scriptures, and in prayers, hymns and spiritual songs there is much material for me to call upon, and I am always thankful for it. Psalm 23 is a favorite because I have it memorized and because when the words come to me, they are sung in a setting written by Charles. The psalm concludes with the lovely promise, *"Surely goodness and mercy shall follow me all the days of my life, and I will dwell in the house of the Lord forever."*

February 23, 2010

We [*the oncologist and I*] visited about all sorts of things, though the question at the core was really "How much longer will I live?" I think this question has been hovering over humanity from the beginning, and we know well that only God knows, but we ask anyway. Jesus says to his disciples, "Can any of you by worrying add a single hour to your span of life? If then you are not able to do so small a thing as that, why do you worry about the rest?" (Luke 12:25–26). It is always the words and wisdom of Scripture and the beauty of the hymns of the faith that carry me onward, so now I become the child again and pray:

> Now the light has gone away;
> Father, listen while I pray,
> Asking Thee to watch and keep
> And to send me quiet sleep.
>
> Jesus, Savior, wash away
> All that has been wrong today;
> Help me ev'ry day to be
> Good and gentle, more like Thee.
>
> Let my near and dear ones be
> Always near and dear to Thee;
> O, bring me and all I love
> To Thy happy home above.[21]

March 30, 2010

Holy Week, and the Church invites everyone to remember again the life-changing events that took place so long ago. Much of the 14th chapter of St. John's Gospel is devoted to Jesus' words of comfort to his disciples as he prepares to depart the Passover supper and enter the Garden of Gethsemane. I particularly like to think of the words, "Let not your heart be troubled, neither let it be afraid" because it addresses directly the hardest part of my own life—that is, the knowing and not-knowing about dying. I think about it a great deal since the arrival of the cancer. Plans are made for the future, but never for a long time, and always with a "maybe" lurking. I am now at the 46th day since the last transfusion; there were 56 days between it and the one prior to that; I hope to continue past Easter before getting another because we are planning a celebratory weekend at the end of April, and the blood is key to having the energy needed. As always, we are optimistic and we look forward to the days ahead. *"Peace I leave with you, my peace I give to you. I do not give to you as the world gives. Do not let your hearts be troubled and do not let them be afraid"* (John 14:27). Have a blessed Easter!

July 20, 2010

Both Janna and John-Paul are here and Heidi is taking time from work to come, too. When we gather, a distinct family trait is that cooking and baking the family recipes seems to calm everyone. There is always some lovely creation beginning or ending in the kitchen. Other calming and lovely things in this difficult year are the incredibly grand flowers that have sprung up in the gardens. One looks at the intricacies of a sunflower and considers the Creator who thought of it for the first time. That act, multiplied more times than can be imagined, presents a picture of what has been woven together into our earthly home. I too am a part of it all, and I accept being fearfully and wondrously made. In the hymn "O God beyond All Praising" the poet speaks most eloquently:

> The flow'r of earthly splendor in time must surely die,
> its fragile bloom surrender to you, the Lord most high;
> but hidden from all nature the eternal seed is sown—
> though small in mortal stature, to heaven's garden grown:
> for Christ, your gift from heaven, from death has set us free,
> and we through him are given / the final victory.[22]

August 11, 2010

We have found the readings from the Psalms to have the cadence of comfort: Psalm 121, Psalm 112, and on and onward. The best prayers seem to come from childhood. "Now I lay me down to sleep, I pray thee Lord my soul to keep. Asking thee to watch and keep, and to send me quiet sleep." Perhaps that prayer repeated hundreds of times throughout this life comforts because here is the same God that made me always feel safe. I think we all had a "pneumonia moment" when we signed the hospice papers, and the fact that I am still here is a happy surprise.

September 10, 2010

What does this ending time feel like? To me, it is feeling sick most of the time, and that is accompanied by the great exhaustion.

The question that hovers over the experience is, "Why?" Those of us who go onward encased in our present bodies ask again and listen carefully. This query must surely be made by humanity all over the world but the answer will not be heard outside of eternity.

Days move forward with the summer's end approaching. For our eyes, it announces itself through the lovely gatherings of dusty pink sedum and the sagging goldenrods that edge our space on every side. Cardinals and blue jays provide some color and the sound of the jay's morning scolds is welcome after a summer season so rich with sound.

I determined to write a short poem for each day that I go forward. Sitting and waiting is too grim. Immediately, I find true poetry is not an easy thing, a fact that has been brought to my attention through vigorous paragraphs in books gotten from the library. Since there is no intent to wave the poems about, I will just write.

And yes, the conversation with God has gotten shrill at times; mostly though, the respite of music that bears beautiful text is always there, and comfort is found. And when one wants to shake a fist, the Psalms provide many good words for outrage and fist-shakings.

* * *

As Connie grew weaker and unable to communicate, her family cared for her in a loving manner, while they shared hymns and psalms with her. Why would this time in her life (or the life of her family) be any different? "Yea, though I walk through the valley of the shadow of death, I will fear no evil; for thou art with me, thy rod and they staff they comfort me" (Psalm 23:4; KJV).

> *Lord, let at last Thine angels come,*
> *To Abr'ham's bosom bear me home,*
> *that I may die unfearing;*
> *And in its narrow chamber keep*
> *My body safe in peaceful sleep*
> *Until thy reappearing.*
> *And then from death awaken me,*
> *That these mine eyes with joy may see,*
> *O Son of God, Thy glorious face,*
> *My Savior and my fount of grace.*

Lord Jesus Christ, my prayer attend, my prayer attend,
And I will praise Thee without end. [23]

No doubt Connie had led this hymn from the organ bench on many occasions. Those words, firmly etched in her mind from years of singing and praying it, became a reality for her on September 16, 2010.

The Reverend Richard C. Eyer (emeritus professor and director of the Concordia Bioethics Institute at Concordia University Wisconsin) wrote that, in the end, it is all Christ. He tells that as his mother-in-law was dying, she was agitated and restless, but the singing of hymns calmed her. After he read portions of Psalm 62 to her, his wife sang "Amazing Grace." Once these words had been sung—"Through many dangers, toils, and snares / I have already come; / His grace has brought me safe thus far, / His grace will lead me home" [24]—she went to be with her Lord. "In the end, it is all Christ . . . from the cross to the resurrection, His cross and ours. In our suffering and dying as His faithful ones, we, too, eventually get to walk through the door with Him!" [25]

Church musicians, hymnody, and spiritual care: the three are related. Hymns nurture the faith and become a part of our being, bringing comfort, peace, and joy in Jesus throughout our lives. Church musicians are charged with leading the singing of such hymns. Hymns provide a special type of spiritual care, giving strength to Christians when no pastor can be present. They help Christians focus on "whatever is true, whatever is noble, whatever is right, whatever is pure, whatever is lovely, whatever is admirable—if anything is excellent or praiseworthy—think about such things. . . . And the God of peace will be with you" (Philippians 4:8–9; NIV).

This is a prayer for church musicians and artists: "God of majesty, whom saints and angels delight to worship in heaven, be with Your servants who make art and music for Your people that with joy we on earth may glimpse Your beauty. Bring us to the fulfillment of that hope of perfection that will be ours as we stand before Your unveiled glory; through Jesus Christ, our Lord." [26] Amen.

Notes

1 The Commission on Worship of The Lutheran Church—Missouri Synod, *Lutheran Service Book* [LSB] (St. Louis: Concordia, 2006), 708, st. 3.

2 Constance Ore, "Writings of Constance Ore (1937–2010)," January 2006, http://www.constanceore.com/2006/01.

3 LSB, prayer 193, p. 311.

4 This is a text from circa 1641 and is set to music by K. Lee Scott (SHADES MOUNTAIN).

5 LSB 818, st. 2.

6 LSB 735, st. 1.

7 LSB 734, st. 4.

8 Emily Dickenson, "'Hope' is the thing with feathers," in *The Poems of Emily Dickinson*, ed. R. W. Franklin (Cambridge, MA: Belknap Press, 1999), 314.

9 *The New Century Hymnal*, ed. Arthur G. Clyde (Cleveland: Pilgrim Press, 1995), 17 (United Church of Christ).

10 LSB 817, st. 6.

11 LSB 543, sts. 3 and 4.

12 LSB 491, st. 1.

13 LSB 878, sts. 1, 4, and 6.

14 LSB 877, sts. 1, 2, and 3.

15 *With One Voice: A Lutheran Resource for Worship* (Minneapolis: Augsburg Fortress, 1995),741, st. 1.

16 Commission on Worship of The Lutheran Church—Missouri Synod, *Lutheran Worship* (St. Louis: Concordia, 1982), 22, sts. 1 and 2.

17 *With One Voice* 669, sts. 1, 2, and 3.

18 LSB 770, st. 1.

19 LSB, p. 258.

20 LSB 886, sts. 1, 3, and 4.

21 LSB 887, sts. 1, 2,and 3.

22 Evangelical Lutheran Church in America, *Evangelical Lutheran Worship* (Minneapolis: Augsburg Fortress, 2006).880, st. 2.

23 LSB 708, st. 3.

24 LSB 744, st. 3.

25 Richard C. Eyer, "In the End, It Is All Christ," The Lutheran Church—Missouri Synod News and Information (5 October 2010), https://blogs.lcms.org/2010/in-the-end-it-is-all-christ-10-2010.

26 LSB, p. 307.

Clockwise from top right: Charles and Connie on their first wedding anniversary, August 14, 1961; Charles and Connie with Dad (Raymond Ore), Christmas 1960; Charles and Connie, 1960; Charles at Connie's home church —"Hanover" Charter Oak, Iowa, where Charles took care of the organ for over 40 years; Charles by the library at Concordia, Seward, May 1996; Connie and Charles celebrating thier 50th wedding anniversary, April 27, 2010.

"When in Our Music God Is Glorified"

Hymns: *Dogma* and *Doxa* in Dialogue

STEPHEN P. STARKE

The year was 1973. I was in my freshman year at Concordia
Junior College in Ann Arbor, MI. Tryouts for Paul Foelber's Concordia
Choir had been posted; I eagerly signed up. The time slot for my
audition arrived and I went to audition before Foelber. I knocked
nervously on his office door and heard his soft-spoken invitation to
enter. He sat at a piano and after a few words of introduction handed me a copy of *The Lutheran Hymnal.* He had me turn to a certain
hymn and asked me to sing the bass line as he played. I could not do
it! I did not know how to read music well enough to accomplish that
simple task! He was very kind about my poor performance. When
the results of the choral auditions were posted, I was not surprised
that I had been assigned to the Concordia Singers, a mixed choir
directed by Harry Gudmundson. In retrospect, I learned a great
deal about music and singing under Gudmundson's leadership and
my two years singing with the Concordia Singers. Upon graduation
from Concordia Junior College with my associate of arts degree in
1975, I transferred to what was then Concordia Teacher's College
in River Forest, IL, for my final two years of higher education. I
auditioned for Thomas Gieschen's mixed choir, the Kapelle, and
happily was accepted. I sang with Gieschen for two wonderful years
and learned a great deal more about sacred music and part-singing.
In 1979 I entered Concordia Theological Seminary in Ft. Wayne,
IN, to study for the pastoral ministry. At the beginning of my second

year, a good friend of mine urged me to try out for the Kantorei. At that time it was a twelve-voice male choir under the direction of Richard Resch. I auditioned and was accepted into that select choir and for two additional, glorious years I learned even more about music. I also learned *the theological implications of what we sing and why that is important.*

Gudmundson. Gieschen. Resch. Three different Concordias. Three very different church musicians and choral directors. Multiple choir tours. Six years of my younger life. What was the common denominator for each choir? *Each choir director stressed the great importance of* what *was being sung!* Yes, choral technique was critical, and such technique occupied much of our rehearsal time; we practiced starting and staying on the correct pitches and blending our voices with unified vocal crescendos and decrescendos. We worked at the constant task of memorizing the music so that we were not visually tied to the printed page. Yet all of this was done solely in service of the sung text, and that for the glory of God.

The things I learned singing in those choirs have crystallized for me these past 30-plus years of both pastoral ministry and hymn writing. I have learned that hymn writers exercise their poetical craft for the very important and pastoral goal of placing words into the mouths of worshippers, words put into service of the Word of God and of the Gospel of our Lord Jesus Christ. Our best hymns are united with our best music so that in our worship God may be glorified. And yet both hymn writers and church musicians recognize that even their best efforts in the area of hymnody and church music still fall far short of the endless, holy hymns of praise sung by saints in the Church Triumphant and by angels in the glory of heaven before the throne of the living God. Thankfully, as with everything else in the life of hymn writers and church musicians, God takes what is offered to him in their text and in their music and he cleanses it with the blood of his Son, so that all of what is offered to God in worship is presented spotless and holy before him, through our Lord Jesus Christ. *Then* in our music God is glorified.

Perhaps a good starting point for what follows is the question, "what is a hymn?" There are many, many different definitions of the word "hymn." I would offer this definition: *a hymn is a com-*

*bination of doctrine (*dogma*) and praise (*doxa*) for worshippers to sing in a corporate setting.* It is good to call to mind the words of the late Lutheran hymn writer, Martin Franzmann: "Theology is Doxology. Theology must sing."[1] How true! Theological substance and churchly music go hand in hand so that God's people can sing words about God as glorious words of praise. Hymns give worshippers a voice of sung response to all that God is and all that God has done. Luther himself modeled this in his day for generations to follow as he placed words into the mouths of the worshippers, words in their own native language. Luther demonstrated the importance of combining the best theology with the best music for the edification of God's people and for the glory of God.

The subtitle of this essay is "Hymns: *Dogma* and *Doxa* in Dialogue." Dialogue plays an important part in hymnody. Many dialogues take place in hymnody and in church music. There is the basic dialogue between the text and the tune so that the music well supports and does not detract in any way from the text and its message.

A great text cannot redeem a poor tune and poor text will not endure, even though it may be wed to a wonderful tune. Text and tune go hand in hand, tune undergirding text and text flowering and bearing fruit through the music to which it has been joined. The proper union of text and tune is a thing of beauty to behold and a thing of joy to sing! One thinks of any number of fine hymns that show the perfect union of text and tune: "For All the Saints" sung to Sine nomine, "Wake, Awake, for Night Is Flying" sung to Wachet auf, "Children of the Heavenly Father" sung to Tryggare kan ingen vara, and so very many more. Perhaps another way of saying this is that there is a critical dialogue between the writer of the hymn text and the composer of the hymn tune.

From the composer's viewpoint, there is a dialogue between the tune and the best and most appropriate setting of that tune. From a performance perspective, there is a dialogue that takes place in worship between the text and the text painting done by the musician or musicians in worship. From the standpoint of a foreign text written in another language, there is a dialogue that takes place between the original language and its translator, guiding the literal translation into a poetical adaptation in another language. However, at the very foundational and most basic level, *a hymn is a theological dialogue between God and his people.* Called out of the darkness of sin and into the marvelous light of Christ, God's people receive the truth that God gives in his Word and then sing that truth back to God as hymns of praise. God then gives his truth, received in faith by believers, and that truth is then directed back to God in hymns of praise, and so this cyclical theological and doxological dialogue continues as this diagram illustrates:

Dogma and *Doxa* in Dialogue[2]

1. God gives his Word. **4. God receives our praise.**

2. *Dogma:* the truths of **3. *Doxa:* praise directed to God**
the Word of God **as we sing back to him**
are received by us. **the truths of his Word.**

The theological dialogue of *dogma* (doctrine) and *doxa* (praise) that takes place within a hymn has four parts. In the first place, everything begins with God, the perfect Giver, as he speaks his Word to us. The apostle James writes, "Every good gift and every perfect gift is from above, coming down from the Father of lights with whom there is no variation or shadow due to change" (James 1:17; ESV). Hymn writing starts with the good and perfect gift of the written Word that has come down to us from God above. To use another image, in Holy Scripture God gives us perfect seed. Hymns are one way in which that perfect seed that God has given is sown into human hearts. We find this comforting promise in Isaiah: "For as the rain and the snow come down from heaven and do not return there but water the earth, making it bring forth and sprout, giving seed to the sower and bread to the eater, so shall my word be that goes out from my mouth; it shall not return to me empty, but it shall accomplish that which I purpose, and shall succeed in the thing for which I sent it" (Isaiah 55:10–11). This author captures this thought in the third stanza of "Hark, the Voice of

Jesus Calling," written in 2001 at the request of the *Lutheran Service Book* project director, Paul Grime:

> For as rain and snow from heaven
> Water seeds in dusty soil,
> Causing them to bud and flower,
> Giving bread to those who toil;
> So the Lord sends forth His promise,
> Words of life and joy and peace—
> Never void to Him returning,
> Bearing fruit with great increase.[3]

Again this understanding is beautifully reflected in the hymn by George W. Briggs, "God Has Spoken by His Prophets":

> God has spoken by His prophets,
> Spoken His unchanging Word;
> Each from age to age proclaiming
> God, the one, the righteous Lord.
> In the world's despair and turmoil,
> One firm anchor holds us fast:
> God is king, His throne eternal;
> God the first, and God the last.
>
> God has spoken by Christ Jesus,
> Christ, the everlasting Son,
> Brightness of the Father's glory,
> With the Father ever one;
> Spoken by the Word Incarnate,
> God of God, before time was;
> Light of light, to earth descending,
> He reveals our God to us.
>
> God is speaking by His Spirit,
> Speaking to our hearts again,
> In the ageless Word declaring
> His own message, now as then.
> Through the rise and fall of nations
> One sure faith yet standing fast;
> God abides, His Word unchanging;
> God the first, and God the last.[4]

The second part of this theological dialogue of *dogma* and *doxa*, a dialogue between God and his people, is this: God's good and perfect Word is received in the human heart. It ought not come as a surprise to any Christians that they receive God's Word *imperfectly*. Christians are simultaneously saint and sinner. Hymn writers and composers are also simultaneously saint and sinner, struggling with issues of ego, pride, inability to receive criticism, envy, and all the rest. As sin sadly mars the tasks of hymn writing and disfigures our lives in many other ways, so also sin clouds and diminishes and undercuts our reception of the Word of God. Because of sin in our lives and in the world around us, we are admonished by God's Word to listen and hear so that the precious seed of God's Word is not snatched away from our hearts by the evil one. The Collect for the Word that is often prayed asks God's blessing as we read, mark, learn, and inwardly digest the Word of God. St. Paul underscores this thought as he writes to the Colossians: "Let the word of Christ dwell in you richly, teaching and admonishing one another in all wisdom, singing psalms and hymns and spiritual songs, with thankfulness in your hearts to God" (Colossians 3:16). We are invited to *dwell* in the Word of God, not just visit it on occasion! It is somewhat overwhelming to comprehend that the Lord God Almighty invites us to live, to take up residence, to settle in and make ourselves at home in his Word! Hymn writers, of all people, must dwell in the Word of God, otherwise their hymns will very likely be devoid of *dogma* or demonstrate a confused *dogma*. Too many hymns contain very little *dogma* or a confused *dogma*. The hymn writer Anna Sophia von Hessen-Darmstadt captures this thought of learning and listening to the Word of God in the first stanza of her text, "Speak, O Lord, Your Servant Listens":

> Speak, O Lord, Your servant listens,
> Let Your Word to me come near;
> Newborn life and spirit give me,
> Let each promise still my fear.
> Death's dread pow'r, its inward strife,
> Wars against Your Word of life;
> Fill me, Lord, with love's strong fervor
> That I cling to You forever![5]

It is important that the Word of God is received by faith within the human heart. Erdmann Neumeister speaks of that importance in the first stanza of his great hymn, "I Know My Faith Is Founded":

> I know my faith is founded
> On Jesus Christ, my God and Lord;
> And this my faith confessing,
> Unmoved I stand on His sure Word.
> Our reason cannot fathom
> The truth of God profound;
> Who trusts in human wisdom
> Relies on shifting ground.
> God's Word is all-sufficient,
> It makes divinely sure;
> And trusting in its wisdom,
> My faith shall rest secure.[6]

The third part of this theological dialogue between God and his people in the form of *dogma* and *doxa* is this: hymn writers take the *dogma* they have received and learned, craft it, and wordsmith it into stanzas of pleasing poetical form. This is done while being conscious of the fact that they are placing words into the mouths of worshippers who will sing them back to God as a hymn of praise. The task of uniting the hymn text to an appropriate tune, and then offering that praise to God, recognizes that the highest praise for God is singing back to God the truth he has first given us. One could think of hymns as a message that says to God, "I have received the truth you have given me in your Word and I praise you for it; I now thankfully return it to you for your glory."

Lutherans understand Christians to be both sinner and saint simultaneously (*simil justus et peccator*). As such, the Christian's praise offered to God is imperfect and will always be imperfect. Yet as we offer our imperfect praise, it is, thankfully, cleansed by the blood of Christ and thus presented before the throne of God as a holy offering completely acceptable to him in Christ. Martin Franzmann perfectly captures some of these thoughts in third stanza of his hymn text "Thy Strong Word":

Thy strong Word bespeaks us righteous;
Bright with Thine own holiness,
Glorious now, we press toward glory,
And our lives our hopes confess.
Alleluia, alleluia!
Praise to Thee who light dost send!
Alleluia, alleluia!
Alleluia without end![7]

These thoughts of the One who comes to us in his Word, in Holy Baptism, and in the Lord's Supper to make us holy are echoed in the fifth stanza of "Christ Sits at God's Right Hand," written by this author in 2002:

Then let us now draw near,
Washed in that precious flood,
And enter the Most Holy Place
By Jesus' blood.
From hearts that are sincere,
Let tongues our hope profess,
And trust anew God's faithful grace
That we confess.[8]

The joyful fourth part of this theological dialogue of *dogma* and *doxa* between God and his people is this: God receives our offerings of praise, cleansed by the blood of Christ! In Christ and through Christ we are bold to approach God. The writer of the book of Hebrews says it this way: "You have come to Mount Zion and to the city of the living God, the heavenly Jerusalem, and to innumerable angels in festal gathering, and to the assembly of the firstborn who are enrolled in heaven, and to God, the judge of all, and to the spirits of the righteous made perfect, and to Jesus, the mediator of a new covenant, and to the sprinkled blood that speaks a better word than the blood of Abel" (Hebrews 12:22–24). The hymn writer Johann Jacob Rimbach speaks of God receiving what we offer to him in the fourth stanza of his hymn text "Baptized into Your Name Most Holy":

All that I am and love most dearly—
Receive it all, O Lord, from me.
Let me confess my faith sincerely;

Help me Your faithful child to be!
Let nothing that I am or own
Serve any will but Yours alone.[9]

The late hymn writer Herman G. Stuempfle expresses the wonder of our God who receives all that we give him in response to his good gifts to us in the fifth stanza of "Voices Raised to You We Offer":

How can any praise we offer
Measure all the thanks we owe?
Take our hearts and hands and voices—
Gifts of love we can bestow.
Alleluia! Alleluia!
Triune God, to You we sing![10]

These thoughts are also captured by Johann Mentzer in the fifth stanza of "Oh, That I Had a Thousand Voices":

Creator, humbly I implore You
To listen to my earthly song
Until that day when I adore You,
Together with the angel throng
And learn with choirs of heav'n to sing
Eternal anthems to my king.[11]

Again, praise offered to Almighty God is captured by this author in the versification of the *Te Deum*, "We Praise You and Acknowledge You, O God," written in 1999:

We praise You and acknowledge You, O God, to be the
    Lord,
The Father everlasting, by all the earth adored.
To You all angel powers cry aloud, the heavens sing,
The cherubim and seraphim their praises to You bring:
"O holy, holy, holy Lord God of Sabaoth;
Your majesty and glory fill the heavens and the earth!"

The band of the apostles in glory sing Your praise;
The fellowship of prophets their deathless voices raise.
The martyrs of Your kingdom, a great and noble throng,

Sing with the holy Church throughout all the world this
    song:
"O all-majestic Father, Your true and only Son,
And Holy Spirit, Comforter—forever Three in One!"

You, Christ, are King of glory, the everlasting Son,
Yet You, with boundless love, sought to rescue ev'ryone:
You laid aside Your glory, were born of virgin's womb,
Were crucified for us and were placed into a tomb;
Then by Your resurrection You won for us reprieve—
You opened heaven's kingdom to all who would believe.

You sit in splendid glory, enthroned at God's right hand,
Upholding earth and heaven by forces You command.
We know that You will come as our Judge that final day,
So help Your servants You have redeemed by blood, we pray;
May we with saints be numbered where praises never end,
In glory everlasting. Amen, O Lord, amen![12]

So to summarize this foundational level of a hymn, a hymn is a
theological dialogue of *dogma* and *doxa* between God and his people. The four points of theological dialogue are these:

1. God is the perfect Giver of the truth of his Word.

2. Hymn writers and composers are imperfect receivers of this
   truth (*dogma*).

3. Hymn writers and composers are imperfect givers of *doxa*
   (praise), who seek to glorify God by singing back to him the
   truth he has first given us.

4. God is the perfect Receiver of our offered hymns, who
   cleanses our offerings of praise to Him by the blood of the
   Lamb who was slain but who is now alive forevermore. *Then,
   in our music, God is glorified!*

The psalmist writes: "The LORD gave the word: great was the
company of those that published it" (Psalm 68:11; KJV). Hymn
writers are, by the grace of God, part of that great company of
preachers, who have received the good and perfect Word given by
God; have read, marked, learned, and inwardly digested that Word;
and have used their God-given gifts to put the truths of God's Word

into a poetic form, placing those truths into the mouths of worshippers to be sung as praise for all that he has done. As the text is being sung, the critical dialogue between text and tune takes place, as the composer's tune supports the text and in no way detracts from it and as the text blossoms and bears fruit by means of the musical contours of note and rhythm within the tune.

To illustrate how this theological dialogue of dogma and *doxa* materializes into a hymn, I offer the example of writing a hymn text based on Psalm 121 (NIV). The psalm reads as follows:

> I lift up my eyes to the hills.
> > From where does my help come?
> My help comes from the LORD
> > who made heaven and earth.
> He will not let your foot be moved;
> > he who keeps you will not slumber.
> Behold, he who keeps Israel
> > will neither slumber nor sleep.
> The LORD is your keeper;
> > the LORD is your shade on your right hand.
> The sun shall not strike you by day,
> > nor the moon by night.
> The LORD will keep you from all evil;
> > he will keep your life.
> The LORD will keep your going out and your coming in
> > from this time forth and forevermore.

Following this pattern mentioned above,

God gives his Word.

Dogma: the truths of the Word of God are received by us.

I reflected upon the words of Psalm 121, yet my reflection and meditation on the Word of God and the truths of this psalm were done in the light of the tune, No Child, by Amanda Husberg, a composer from Brooklyn, NY. The dialogue between text and tune is quite important to me, and I have found in my hymn writing that having a particular tune in mind not only sets the tone for the text, but enables the hymn to place emphasis on certain words, emphasis that is underscored by the notes in the tune. Not only that, No Child has a depth of feeling connected to the notes that made it a good choice for the text as it was being written. Psalm 121 speaks of God's providential care and the believer's trust in that care. The resulting hymn text was "I Lift My Eyes to See":

> I lift my eyes to see
> The mountains soar and tower—
> How strong my Maker's power!
> How sure His help for me!
>
> God keeps your footsteps true;
> His eye is never sleeping,
> His Israel ever keeping—
> So great His love for you!
>
> God guards you by His might;
> The burning sunlight shading
> And when its glow is fading,
> God keeps you safe at night.
>
> At times of trial and strife,
> When evil foes assail you,
> God's presence will not fail you—
> The Lord preserves your life!
>
> When you walk out the door,
> To where your path may lead you,
> God's blessing will precede you,
> Both now and evermore.
>
> All laud and glory be
> To Father, Son, and Spirit,
> Through whom we life inherit—
> O blesséd Trinity![13]

The dialogue of *dogma* and *doxa* is reflected in this pattern below, as the praise offered to God in "I Lift My Eyes to See" to the tune No Child is received by God, cleansed by the blood of Christ, and presented holy before God's throne:

God receives our praise.

Doxa: **praise directed to God
as we sing back to him the truths of his Word.**

Here is another example to illustrate this theological dialogue between *dogma* and *doxa* that takes place in this author's hymn text, "The Tree of Life." The foundational thought for this text was in the proper preface for Passion: "On the tree of the cross You gave salvation to mankind that, whence death arose, thence life also might rise again and that he who by a tree once overcame likewise by a tree might be overcome, through Jesus Christ our Lord."[14] As I stood at the altar praying these words within the Divine Service, my mind had a momentary detour: "this would be a great starting point for a hymn!" In the days that followed, I thought about the truths of God's Word surrounding humanity's fall into sin and the promised Seed of the woman, who on the cross of Calvary crushed the serpent's head. Reflecting on such texts from Holy Scripture as Genesis 2:9; Genesis 3:1–7, 15; John 3:16; and Rev. 22:2, this strong and overarching truth came to mind: *the cross is our tree of life in this world*!

God gave his Word. The truth (*dogma*) was received. My goal as a hymn writer was then to place those truths about Christ's redemptive work into a pleasing poetical form, so that those truths could edify the worshipper and also be sung back to God as praise (*doxa*). The tune I had in mind as I wrote this text was an Irish Christmas tune, The Wexford Carol. The text has since been wed to the fine tune by Bruce W. Becker, Tree of Life. Here are the four stanzas of this text, "The Tree of Life":

The tree of life with every good
In Eden's holy orchard stood,
And of its fruit so pure and sweet
God let the man and woman eat.
Yet in this garden also grew
Another tree, of which they knew;
Its lovely limbs with fruit adorned
Against whose eating God had warned.

The stillness of that sacred grove
Was broken, as the serpent strove
With tempting voice Eve to beguile
And Adam too by sin defile.
O day of sadness when the breath
Of fear and darkness, doubt and death,
Its awful poison first displayed
Within the world so newly made.

What mercy God showed to our race,
A plan of rescue by His grace:
In sending One from woman's seed,
The One to fill our greatest need—
For on a tree uplifted high
His only Son for sin would die,
Would drink the cup of scorn and dread
To crush the ancient serpent's head!

Now from that tree of Jesus' shame
Flows life eternal in His name;
For all who trust and will believe,
Salvation's living fruit receive.
And of this fruit so pure and sweet
The Lord invites the world to eat,
To find within this cross of wood
The tree of life with every good.[15]

To once more illustrate the dialogue that takes place between text and tune in a hymn, I offer the text "There Is a Time for Everything," to the tune St. Peter's Norwalk by composer Stephen Johnson of New York. As the one-year anniversary of 9/11 approached, I was asked by the Commission on Worship of the Missouri Synod to write a hymn to mark the first anniversary of this national tragedy. Since I firmly believe that a hymn text needs to be anchored in the Word of God, I began to reflect on different sections of Holy Scripture: Ecclesiastes 3:1–8, Genesis 30:20, Romans 8:28, 1 Corinthians 13:12, and others. In addition, since I also firmly believe that the dialogue between text and tune is so critical, I began to reflect upon these words in the light of Johnson's tune (which he had actually composed for the text above, "The Tree of Life"). The tune suggested a direction for the text, and the tune also had the depth and range of feeling necessary for such a hymn text. This is the resulting hymn text:

> There is a time for ev'rything,
> A time for all that life may bring:
> A time to plant, a time to reap,
> A time to laugh, a time to weep,
> A time to heal, a time to slay,
> A time to build where rubble lay,
> A time to die, a time to mourn,
> A time for joy and to be born,
>
> A time to hold, then be alone,
> A time to gather scattered stone,
> A time to break, a time to mend,
> A time to search and then to end,
> A time to keep, then throw away,
> A time to speak, then nothing say,
> A time for war till hatreds cease,
> A time for love, a time for peace.
>
> Eternal Lord, Your wisdom sees
> And fathoms all life's tragedies;
> You know our grief, You hear our sighs—
> In mercy, dry our tear-stained eyes.
> From evil times, You bring great good;
> Beneath the cross, we've safely stood.
> Though dimly now life's path we trace,
> One day we shall see face to face.

Before all time had yet begun,
You, Father, planned to give Your Son;
Lord Jesus Christ, with timeless grace,
You have redeemed our time-bound race;
O Holy Spirit, Paraclete,
Your timely work in us complete;
Blest Trinity, Your praise we sing—
There is a time for ev'rything![16]

In summary, a hymn is a theological dialogue of *dogma* and *doxa* between God and his people. Then in our music God is glorified! Yes, to God alone be the glory! The words of Norman Nagel from the introduction to *Lutheran Worship* offer a fine conclusion to hymns as dogma and *doxa* in dialogue:

> Our Lord speaks and we listen. His Word bestows on us what it says. Faith that is born from what is heard acknowledges the gifts received with eager thankfulness and praise. Music is drawn in this thankfulness and praise, enlarging and elevating the adoration of our gracious giver God.
>
> Saying back to him what he has said to us, we repeat what is most true and sure. Most true and sure is his name, which he put on us with the water of our Baptism. We are his. This we acknowledge at the beginning of the Divine Service. Where his name is, there is he. Before him we acknowledge that we are sinners, and we plead forgiveness. His forgiveness is given us, and we, freed and forgiven, acclaim him as our great and gracious God as we apply to ourselves the words he has used to make himself known to us.
>
> The rhythm of our worship is from him to us, and then from us back to him. He gives his gifts, and together we receive and extol them. We build one another up as we speak to one another psalms, hymns, and spiritual songs. . . . We are heirs of an astonishing rich tradition. Each generation receives from those who went before and, in making that tradition . . . its own, adds what

best may serve in its own day—the living heritage and something new.[17]

When in our music God is glorified
And adoration leaves no room for pride,
It is as though the whole creation cried:
Alleluia!

How often, making music, we have found
A new dimension in the world of sound
As worship moved us to a more profound
Alleluia!

So has the church, in liturgy and song,
In faith and love, through centuries of wrong,
Borne witness to the truth in ev'ry tongue:
Alleluia!

And did not Jesus sing a psalm that night
When utmost evil strove against the light?
Then let us sing, for whom he won the fight:
Alleluia!

Let ev'ry instrument be tuned for praise;
Let all rejoice who have a voice to raise;
And may God give us faith to sing always:
Alleluia![18]

Yes, to God alone be the glory!

Sing, morning stars, as when God scored creation;
Saints, laud the Lamb whose blood has robed your throng;
Come, Christians, praise, with Spirit-wrought elation—
Exalt the triune God through endless song![19]

Notes

1   Martin Franzmann, quoted in Richard N. Brinkley, *Thy Strong Word: The Enduring Legacy of Martin Franzmann* (St. Louis: Concordia, 1993), 36.

2   Stephen P. Starke, "Hymns: Dogma and Doxa: A Dialogue" (paper presented at Institute of Liturgy, Preaching, and Church Music, Seward, NE, 28–31 July 2014).

3   The Commission on Worship of The Lutheran Church—Missouri Synod, *Lutheran Service Book* [LSB] (St. Louis: Concordia, 2006), 827.

4 LSB 583.

5 LSB 589.

6 LSB 587.

7 LSB 578.

8 Stephen P. Starke, *O Sing of Christ: The Hymns of Stephen P. Starke* (St. Louis: Concordia, 2005), 57.

9 LSB 590.

10 LSB 795.

11 LSB 811.

12 Starke, *O Sing of Christ*, 120.

13 Stephen P. Starke, "I Lift My Eyes to See," 7 December 2010, http://starkekirchenlieder.blogspot.com/2010/12/i-lift-my-eyes-to-see.html.

14 Commission on Worship of The Lutheran Church—Missouri Synod, *Lutheran Worship* [LW] (St. Louis: Concordia, 1982), p. 147.

15 *Evangelical Lutheran Hymnary* (St. Louis: MorningStar, 1996), 302.

16 Starke, *O Sing of Christ*, 97.

17 LW, p. 6.

18 Bernard Braley, *The Hymns and Ballads of Fred Pratt Green* (Carol Stream, IL: Hope, 1982), 51–52.

19 Stephen P. Starke, "Ring, Bells! Ring Out the Message of Salvation" (hymn written for the 50th anniversary of the St. Lorenz Mixed Choir, Frankenmuth, MI, 2007), st. 5.

The Church Musician and the World

CHRISTOPHER S. AHLMAN

"The Church Musician and the World." That's quite a title. To be perfectly honest, I've never seen it before in any kind of literature either pertinent to or related to church music, much less seen the general concept that it reflects. Other titles of a much less global scope, such as "The Church Musician and the Parish" or "The Church Musician and the Church," would be more usual. But "The Church Musician and the World" it is, and "The Church Musician and the World" it will be.

Given the magnitude of the scope of the topic, where does one even begin? One could simply begin by dissecting the title into the inevitable two parts, and then proceed to either (1) take up the task of describing (or, perhaps, prescribing) who church musicians were, are, or would be, along with describing how the world as we have thus far known it, know it currently, and either deem it or hope it to be is related to church musicians and what they have to offer; or (2) endeavor unto futility to describe "the world" and then, somehow, proceed to set forth the church musician's role in that grand land of abstracted nonreality—which would (in some way) likely end up as something little more than a high-brow nostalgic lament over some sort of departure from some set of "glory days" that glows more intensely even as it perhaps glows more dimly. Neither option sounds very promising, at least to me.

There is another way to begin, thankfully. This way is one that is prompted, to say the very least, by the confessional tradition in which both Charles Ore and I have found ourselves—granted, in both disparate and coterminous stages in its more-recent history; a tradition not only itself begun by the Word of the Lord but also a tradition that, when it is truly at its best, itself goes about its business beginning (and continuing, and eventually ending) with the Word of the Lord. To that end, I have taken the liberty of providing treatments of three scriptural texts designated by a contingent within the Church catholic—in this instance, The Episcopal Church—for the liturgical commemoration on July 28 of Johann Sebastian Bach, Georg Friedrich Handel, and Henry Purcell: three significant figures, to be sure, whose sacred works still hallow countless churchly spheres in this world of ours. While each treatment is directly pertinent to the text immediately preceding it, and while each treatment possesses a different predominant character (i.e., exegetical, historical), all three treatments should be considered as part of a larger single overall treatment that is homiletical, reflective, and honorific in overall approach, where seeming literary and conceptual disparity converges in harmonious confluence—and that occurring, as it will be seen, in surprising ways.

It is my hope and prayer that, on the occasion of his 80th birthday, this essay will serve to pay fitting tribute to Charles and his life, his career, and his legacy, and thus serve as an adequate expression of thanks to Almighty God in Christ Jesus through the Holy Spirit for Charles, through whom countless people have been blessed.

> 2 Chronicles 7:1–6:[1]
>
> 1 When Solomon was bringing completion to the prayer, fire rained from the heavens and consumed the burnt-offering and the slaughter-sacrifice, and the glory of YHWH[2] filled the temple.
>
> 2 And the priests were not able to enter to the house of YHWH, for the glory of YHWH filled the temple of YHWH.
>
> 3 And all the children of Israel, having seen the fire and the glory of YHWH upon the temple, bent the knee to the pavement with faces to the ground, and they worshipped and gave thanks unto YHWH: "For he is good, for his mercy is unto eternity."

4 Then the king and all the people offered the sacrifice before the face of YHWH.

5 And the king, Solomon, sacrificed the twenty-two thousand oxen and the one hundred twenty thousand flocks. Thus he dedicated the house of God—the king and all the people.

6 And the priests were standing according to their offices,[3] also the Levites with all the accompanimental instruments[4] of YHWH, which David, the king, made for the liturgical-musical giving of thanks[5] unto YHWH—for his mercy is unto eternity—in the praises of David by their hand, and the priests with trumpets[6] in front of them, and all Israel were standing.

Even in the regular encounter with the text of sacred Scripture, the evident priorities of the scriptural writers can strike one as a bit curious to some degree, at least initially. This is no less the case with the priests and Levites and their involvement with musical performance at the dedication of the Temple, as relayed by the Chronicler. Aside from brief references to musical instruments themselves that were present and utilized at the dedication, musical details (along with details of various other kinds) are scarce. As a result the reader must certainly (and, at least with the exercises in this contribution, *will* certainly) delve more deeply into the immediate, approximate, and more remote contexts of sacred Scripture in order to arrive at the best picture of how the dedication of the Temple and, more specifically, the musical performance part thereof took form. That being said, however, the Chronicler's account of the musical expression and performance involved in the dedication of the Temple in essence leaves the reader rather wanting for such detail—at least to those who, in some way, either take interest at some level or are directly and intensely involved in the music that is present at the liturgical ritual of the people of God. The Chronicler renders other aspects of the event much more prominent.

One of these prominent aspects, however and thankfully, is indeed pertinent to said musical performance, namely, the aspect of *place* and *position*—both that of the musician priests and Levites and also, in a more happenstance manner of acknowledgment, that of the people of Israel in proximity to the dedication ceremony. This aspect is not exclusively a matter of some "point on a map" of the Temple blueprints; rather, this is a much more comprehensive matter of "place" or "position," namely, that of a "charge to fulfill," an "order to carry out," and still further, with all the muster that we can extract, of "delineated offices in which to serve." This then would naturally correspond to an actual spatial assignment and physical positioning from which the pitches and rhythms and timbres would ring. For the Chronicler, when it comes to the relaying of the dedication of the Temple itself, what is most important to know—and thus to record and thereby convey—is that the priests and Levites (as well as the people of Israel themselves) have a holistic *place* and *position*, a locative ceremonial charge, a cultic office to hold and to fulfill, itself given clear directive from David the king[7]—a directive given, according to the Chronicler, in line with divine mandate.[8] Such importance is recognized, confirmed, and advanced here in the text at hand and subsequently elsewhere[9] by the translators of the Septuagint, who render the Hebrew *al-mishmerotham* as *tas phylakas*:[10] "keeping their charge," "fulfilling their office," and the like.

All of this might strike most (if not all) of us as a bit odd, if not also rather unnecessary. The Chronicler is, however, of a different mind than most (if not all) of us, at least on this particular occasion. For the Chronicler, it is completely natural, logical, and indeed necessary to highlight the aspect of the Temple musicians holding and fulfilling their office and charge. It signifies that there is a musical "place," a "spot," an "office," consisting of time and space, instituted by David himself and carved out just for the Temple musicians, a signification that, for the reader, serves as the prime mover for a grander external entailment.

- The essential and necessary office and charge of the Temple musician entails that there is both a means by and an occasion for which such office and charge are carried out and thus fulfilled, namely (in this instance), by means of the accompanimental instruments made at David's command for the communal thanksgiving of the people of Israel.

- Such essential and necessary means of—and occasion for—the discharge of the office entails that there must be a physical place where such office and such thanksgiving is to occur, namely, the Temple itself.
- Such essential and necessary physical place is a necessary extension of that which provides its raison d'être, namely, the altar of burnt offering.
- The essential and necessary altar of burnt offering is premised upon the activity that occasions it, namely, the sacrifice of the burnt offering.
- The reality that is the sacrifice of burnt offering, in totality, itself stems from the mandate of YHWH, accompanied by divine promise.[11]

All of which is to say, in reverse, that where the mandate and promise of the Lord enter time and space in form and shape, there you have an altar, and thus a building, thus a people, thus a ritually realized thanksgiving, thus a musical expression thereof, thus a musical means thereunto, thus a *musician*. Put more succinctly, where God does his thing in the world, it is necessary that there also be musicians to do their thing in the world, namely, to realize the Church's thanksgiving in the world—with all the prophesying that cymbals, harps, lyres, and so forth can provide.[12]

Yes, you read that correctly: "prophesying"—another curious descriptor that the Chronicler attaches (albeit a bit earlier on in his account) to the whole scenario of the office and charge of the priestly and Levitical church musicians in general and to the means by which they fulfilled their office in particular:

> And David and the chiefs of the whole host set apart unto the service the sons of Asaph and of Heman and of Jeduthun, those prophesying by means of[13] lyres, by means of lutes, and by means of clashing cymbals, and the number of them, the people of employment unto their service, was: unto the sons of Asaph: Zaccur and Joseph, and Nethaniah, and Asharelah—sons of Asaph, under the directive hand of Asaph, the prophet under the directive hand of the king; unto Jeduthun, the sons of

Jeduthun: Gedaliah, Zeri, Jeshaiah, Shimei, Hashabiah, and Mattithiah—six under the directive hand of their father Jeduthun, the prophet by means of the lyre unto the giving of thanks and praise unto YHWH.[14]

Such prophesying is not of the "foretelling" sort, but rather of the "forthtelling" sort, confirmed by the rendering of *tous apophtheg-gomenous* in the Septuagint: "those declaring by way of acoustical expression," an adjective that conveys the reality—and thus the genuine challenge—that such declaration had the aspect of sound and its various components and tenets at the forefront of its immediate concern.[15] The content of the forthtelling was so pre-eminent and mattered so much that it merited "second place," so to speak, to the immediate concern and industry of the musical prophets, the "forth-tellers." The matter of forthtelling was nothing short of urgent, meaning that nothing short of aural boldness and loudness would do, meaning therefore that nothing less than an exclusive focus and employment upon this acoustical declaration would do.

Such forthtelling prophecy, such fulfilling of office and charge, certainly hearkens back far beyond the occasioning of the Temple and its precursor sites during the kingdom of David and Solomon, back through the kingdom of Saul, the period of the Judges, the period of Israelite conquest, and even back through the period of wilderness wandering. It hearkens as far back as Miriam the prophetess, who "forthtold" by means of tambourine and dance. Additionally, such prophecy and fulfilling of office and charge hearkens forward, through and beyond the divided kingdom and its great periods of adversity, through and beyond the decline and ultimate exile of Judah, through and beyond the period of both Judean returns from exile and restoration—along with those many struggles—to the appointed time: when Jesus, who by divine mandate and with divine promise handed himself over on our behalf "as an offering and sacrifice to God unto fragrant odor";[16] who serves not only as the point, in time and space, of acceptable spiritual sacrifice but also as the edifice-extension of that point and that activity;[17] who, in his place and position as our great High Priest, through the means of complete obedience and suffering unto death, resolutely carried out his orders and fulfilled his charge[18]—producing a salvific cacophony of pitches and rhythms and timbres that truly leaves none of us wanting for detail.

Hence the Chronicler's curious details, which in the end strike church musicians as strangely familiar—if not also natural, logical, and indeed necessary—as they hold and fulfill their office and charge in this grand context where God is doing his thing, and the Church her thing, in the world.

Colossians 2:.2–6:

2 . . . in order that their hearts will be consoled, having been united in love and to every abundance of the certainty of the conscience, unto a knowledge of the mystery of God, Christ,

3 in whom are all the treasures of wisdom and hidden things of knowledge.

4 This I say, in order that no one might delude you in the art of persuasion.

5 For even if I am absent in the flesh, I am nevertheless present with you in spirit, rejoicing and seeing from you the good order and the firmness of your faith in Christ.

6 Therefore, as you received Christ the Lord, walk about in him.

Church musicians normally do not consider themselves to be rhetoricians, but they really ought to do so, because that is precisely who they are. In various aspects of their work—performance, composition, service planning, and so forth—church musicians are, in a very real way, engaged in the art of rhetoric: the art of strategic placement for the sake of crafting and then delivering an argument, for the purposes of grabbing their hearers' attention, ultimately convincing them by means of logical devices of the "point" being made, with the ultimate goal of motivating their hearers toward consequent action. Indeed, the vocation of the church musician in indeed a far cry from "showing up to play"; rather, it is much closer to the reality of "calling to arms."

To some—perhaps to many—such may be found to be far too odd, if not saying far too much altogether. To this contingent church musicians serve primarily, if not exclusively, a supportive role to those assembled at the liturgical assembly, a role centered primarily, if not exclusively, on congregational song. Thus the personification of church musician as ones "calling the congregation to arms" flirts with the fanciful at the very least and leans toward the absurd at the utmost. To them church musicians are more the musical facilitators of the Divine Service—ones with insightful interpretive capabilities, to be sure, that ably manifest themselves in such realities as registration choice, conscious text-painting of strophic content via judicious use of alternate harmonizations, strategic utilization of the choir, and supplemental or alternate (or both) instrumentation, and so on. For some—perhaps for many—the concept of the church musician as an orator is a rather foreign one.

Yet as time progresses and research discovers more, such a concept becomes less and less foreign, and as a result the personification of the church musician becomes less exclusively one of a "facilitator" and indeed much more one of a rhetorical master—even a "change agent" of sorts. Considering the musical history of the Western hemisphere alone, such really should come as little surprise, if not none altogether, given:

- the emphasis given to phrasing and text declamation in the creation and further cultivation of plainsong throughout much of the medieval period;
- both the rediscovery of ancient Greek thought on (among many other topics) word-music relationships and musical affect and the focused utilization of syntax and cadence in compositional shape that arose in the grand humanistic milieu of the fifteenth and sixteenth centuries;
- the impulse in the Baroque compositional mind to utilize then-conventional musical gestures of various sorts to imitate, to dramatize, and thus to convey influence, power, and emotion, along with the consequential impulse to codify rhetorical-musical figures

in order to more fully understand and advance the art;

- the proclivity of musical theorists of the Classical period to analyze melodic form in terms of sentential structure; and

- undoubtedly a plethora of examples more approximate to our time. Rhetoric is, in more ways than one, part and parcel of the musical endeavor.

Such is unquestionably the case when one considers church music that has manifested itself within Lutheran ecclesiastical circles, in particular that of the compositional activity of Dietrich Buxtehude and later J. S. Bach, among many other contemporaries—a period of time that was a veritable zenith of the genre, unparalleled to date. Such compositional activity was in essentially every respect a symptomatic reality of a greater underlying rhetorical root, one that pervaded nearly every aspect of cultural and intellectual life in northern Germany in the wake of the Reformation, thanks to the educational reforms of the humanist rhetorician Philipp Melanchthon. Dietrich Bartel gives us a brief glimpse of such a milieu:

All course instruction was conducted in Latin. Furthermore, all conversation, whether in the classroom or on the playground, was to be in Latin. (Although the exclusive concentration on Latin abated throughout the seventeenth century, it was not until the eighteenth century that the vernacular replaced Latin as the language of rhetoric.) Introductory rhetoric was only taught in the final one or two years of school, after the students had thoroughly mastered Latin grammar and syntax. The weekly curriculum of the advanced students included eight hours of Latin, three hours of dialectic (logic), two hours of rhetoric, and two hours of Cicero. In addition to other subjects, provision was also made for further private tutoring in rhetoric. The student was taught to prepare a given topic either in oral or written form according to the examples of classical authors. To this end the student used various textbooks which presented the general rhetorical concepts and techniques of the classical authors (Aristotle, Cicero, Quintilian) in a condensed form. . . . Rules of rhetoric were defined with examples from classical writings, providing material which the students could emulate. Classical authors were not read for their literary content but rather to determine linguistic rules. Like all other disciplines including Latin grammar and music, the subject of rhetoric was taught through *praeceptum, exemplum, et imitatio* [rule, example, and imitation].[19]

Eventually, as growing musical-liturgical needs arose within north German Lutheran circles—needs that were provided for, in large part, by the reciprocating musical force of *Lateinschule* ("Latin school") pupils—the discipline of music then paralleled rhetoric in terms of importance. This resulted in the near fusion of the disciplines of rhetoric and music, to the point that the discipline of musical composition became "rhetoricized" in nature. Again, Bartel provides helpful commentary:

Through the introduction of Lutheran liturgical practices, greater emphasis was placed on congregational involvement, which was realized musically primarily through the many new Lutheran chorales. Luther's theology of music also encouraged the inclusion of polyphonic choral music in the liturgy, with the choral leadership in the churches provided by the various parochial school choirs. Music was thereby given a greatly increased significance in both the liturgy and in the church's school curriculum. Simultaneously, the role and position of the *Kantor*, who directed the church choirs and taught music at the schools, also rose in stature. . . . With the growing humanist interest in the classics and the increased significance of practical music-making in the parochial schools, the place of music in the liberal arts underwent an important change: while *musica speculativa* [speculative music] began to disappear from curricula, the applied musical discipline was promoted to a position comparable to the linguistic arts, becoming part of the core curriculum of the Lutheran *Lateinschulen*. Rhetoric would provide a paradigm for its sister discipline, music. In accordance with Luther's teaching, music itself was regarded as a heightened form of speech, becoming a rhetorical sermon in sound. Through the *Lateinschule* curriculum, rhetorical terminology and methodology was already familiar to student and teacher alike, expediting the musical adaptation of rhetorical terminology and concepts. In adopting ancient and distinguished rhetorical terminology and methods, the art of musical composition was given both a greater legitimacy and a clearly established rationale and objective.[20]

Such rationale and objective—namely, the ordered, persuasive communication via the control, reflection, and arousal of human passions through the artistic treatment of musical-rhetorical figures (the identical modus operandi of sermon preparation)—was initially championed and advanced most prominently via the musical treatises of Joachim Burmeister, to be followed by those of Athanasius Kircher and, still later, Johann Matheson.[21]

It must be said that the intentional rhetorical training of those who would become church musicians (and, more broadly, of those progressing through a more-or-less standard middle school and high school experience, which eventually leads toward university preparation) does in no way compare, unfortunately, with the standard rhetorical, and then musical-rhetorical, regimen commonplace throughout northern Germany of the seventeenth and eighteenth centuries. Nevertheless, it must be asserted that the rhetorical stature and capability that the church musician holds and, yes, wields—for good or for ill—should come as no surprise whatsoever to anyone, given the grand church music legacy in which we—in our current day, to some extent—still stand: concerning which we either employ our skill and industry or experience with some regularity as we gather with the people of God where God himself in Christ through the Holy Spirit has promised to be found. Truly, anyone with any sort of contact with church music owes it to themselves to be both honest and candid with the reality that rhetoric—the "art of persuasion"—is indeed inseparable from musical performance within the liturgical gathered assembly—and to be honest and candid not simply for the sake of being so, as wonderful as those traits and postures are for church music, for the Church, and for life in general. Rather, also and most importantly, doing so for the sake of guarding the Church against delusion, of serving as an agent of unity in love and of abundant certainty of the conscience, and thus ultimately standing as a regular and steadfast harbinger of consolation for the Church, bringing it ever unto the knowledge of the mystery of God who is none other than Christ Jesus himself.

It truly is not the case that the Apostle Paul found rhetorical activity and display to be innately delusion-inducing. The accounts of his orations in the Acts of the Apostles, along with the Pauline epistles themselves and the progression of content that they set forth, make it abundantly clear to anyone in sympathetic readership with such writings that such was simply not the case. Rather, rhetoric was a crucial means by which the people of God—in this instance, the Church in Colossae and Laodicea—were *consoled*, which is why Paul, out of his sheer agony over the Colossian and Laodicean Christians concerning this very aim and goal, put pen to paper. Paul knew that if consolation was to take place, things would need to get rhetorical and, by means of a simple rhetorical swipe of nothing more (and nothing less) than an inferential particle, a referent of premise, and a mandate, consolation was secured: "Therefore, as you received Christ the Lord, walk about in him." With such a baptismal premise and all the glorious promises that rest upon it, the implication by way of inference and mandate only seal and confirm such a reality, leaving the readership with that which Paul agonized so mightily to see through: consolation, a comfort beyond tangible measure, in which to go about the consequent action of walking about freely to and fro.

No matter the level of intentional training in rhetoric—a discipline with which the church musician is in a real and tangible way already relatively familiar—that is the gift, task, and privilege of church musicians, no matter the situation in which they find themselves: to beckon the Church and "call it to arms" through all of the persuasive arts at their disposal—at times out of the depths of sheer agony—out of the delusion that so besets the Church in this broken world from age to age, from century to century, and into the consolation of Christ in the context of love and in certainty in the truth. That is something that facilitation—"showing up to play"—simply cannot do and thus ought not to do. That is something that is anything but odd or foreign. And for all of this, ultimately, we simply cannot thank God enough!

Luke 2:8–14:

8 And shepherds were in the countryside, living in the fields and guarding their flocks at the watch of the night.

9 And an angel of the Lord stood near them and the glory of the Lord shone around them, and they were terrified with great fear.

10 And the angel said to them, "Do not be afraid, for, behold, I announce you a great joy, which will be for all the people,

11 for today a Savior, who is Christ the Lord, has been born unto you in the city of David.

12 And this is a sign for you: you will find the infant itself wrapped in clothes and lying in a manger."

13 And, suddenly, a multitudinous army of heaven came with the angel, praising God and saying:

14 "Glory in the highest to God and peace upon the earth among people of goodwill."

It is rather remarkable that, even in the most seemingly variegated and surreal of scenarios, diverse trajectories converge and real and discernible patterns and consistencies emerge when endeavors are taken up once again, and where there's a fair amount of shoulder-rubbing in the process. Serving as an excellent example of this is the evangelist Luke, who states from the outset of his Gospel account:

Since many have attempted to repeat in proper order
a narrative concerning the deeds that themselves stand
fulfilled among us, even as those eyewitnesses and ser-

vants from the beginning handed over the happenings of the word, it seemed also to me to write for you—accurately, in order—a course of events again concerning everything, most noble Theophilus, in order that you might know concerning the words of certainty, of which are taught.[22]

For Luke, an accurate and orderly course of events concerning everything that stands fulfilled with respect to the person and work of Jesus Christ—and thus everything that is contained in such a course of events—is ultimately about and vital to *certainty*. This includes, to be sure, those events occurring prior to Jesus' earthly ministry that the other three canonical evangelists themselves also found necessary to include, in one form or another, in their own gospel accounts: the arrival of John the Baptizer as the precursor of the Jesus the Lord[23] and then his messianic preaching,[24] which together found their culmination in the baptism of Jesus,[25] to reference only a brief collective example. It includes those events or realities from the same approximate period of time that one or both of the other Synoptic Gospel writers themselves deemed worthy of recounting: the genealogy of Jesus,[26] the brief allusion to the general childhood of Jesus,[27] John the Baptizer's preaching of repentance[28] and subsequent imprisonment,[29] and the temptation of Jesus.[30] But also, and perhaps most importantly, it includes those events that only Luke (perhaps for a veritable host of reasons) included. Several of these come at the reader at the beginning of his account, immediately following his exordium of sorts to the most excellent Theophilus: the announcement of the birth of John the Baptizer,[31] the Annunciation,[32] the Visitation,[33] the birth of John the Baptist,[34] the birth of Jesus,[35] the angelic announcement to the shepherds of the arrival of the birth of Jesus,[36] the circumcision and presentation of the infant Jesus in the Temple[37]—truly necessary, salvific events. All of these hinge, as Tertullian was so prone to say, "on the flesh,"[38] that is, on the incarnation of the Son of God as human being in the person of Jesus, the very event that brought certainty to the words that gave witness unto it, words that in turn gave certainty to those who heard them.

And there is where the reader finds the shepherds in the countryside, as they are "fulfilling the discharge of their place and office in life" (as Luke, like the Chronicler, endeavors so acutely to render for his readership): in a place where certainty unlike any other is at hand. All of a sudden, in the context of and in the midst of their very place and position in life, the shepherds find themselves quite approximate to that incarnational event of certainty. This then became known to them by means of forthtelling words that deliver not only the very certainty from which they derive but also deliver with stunning efficiency an implicit mandate and call to action that orators themselves are at pains to achieve. And before the heralding angel can catch a breath—and before the shepherds, unlike their precursors in the Lukan narrative, can squeeze in any semblance of a question—there appears a countless army of angelic beings, fulfilling their own offices and charges by way of uttering an *Exclamatio* beyond even Cicero's wildest dreams.

What remained for the shepherds, of course, was then indeed to act, to follow through upon the certainty given to them via words, to encounter for themselves in "the flesh" this reality upon which all reality and all certainty and all words hang. But there was more: the shepherds, who entered into this reality of certainty by way of words of certainty, then brought others into the same reality by way of the same means, and then brought these same others unto sheer and utter astonishment as to what exactly had taken place.[39]

If church music in this world is anything—and it indeed is many things all at once—it is this: a context, a meeting place, even a portal (if one will) that assumes within itself the various places and positions and offices and charges of this world, and those who hold them, in close proximity to a *certainty* unlike any other—a God who has taken on flesh, who has become inseparable from this world to the point of embracing all of its created nature and redeeming its fallen qualities. It is a means by which—through concentrated tones, timbres, textures, rhythms, meters, phrases, periods, and the like, along with intentional invention, arrangement, and delivery—words beget the same incarnational certainty from which they arise and emerge. It is a vehicle by which divine mandates are enacted and then considered, planned, and acted upon in sheer and uninhibited joy in the various places and positions of life in which people find themselves, resulting in their ultimate astonishment at the certainty that is at hand.

Thus, if church musicians are anyone—and indeed they are, often many people all at once, so to speak—they are the heralds fulfilling their office and charge, employing the innate gifts and capabilities that they possess, with the end that divine words deliver divine certainty to those within divine proximity. They are the ones who play an indispensable role in rousing people to unquestioned action, leading to the sheer marvel of still others. They are the ones who, after marshaling everything at their disposal, find themselves without a sufficient opportunity to catch a breath before the inevitable exclamations—both small and great—begin to realize themselves in fleshly form.

The many of us who have come from contrastive landscapes and histories and perspectives and priorities—and perhaps even the most surreal of circumstances—and have converged upon the places where Charles was present and active would themselves find, I have no doubt, that real and discernible patterns and consistencies emerged when endeavors were (and are) taken up with him. Many and various, yet regular and consistent, composers of high quality and endurance and conceptual resonance with the incarnational certainty would be represented among members of the organ studio. These would thus constantly sound forth their music through the doors of organ practice rooms and the chapel and recital halls and then ultimately emerge in recital programs, to the delight of many in the community. Encountering one improvisation after another from Charles' mind and then hands and feet would inevitably soon lead to an extension in that grand exercise of "repetition-variation-contrast" among the many captivated yet nascent "eager-beaver" organ students, testing their "chops" as the personal reservoir of confidence allowed in private (or as the hymn-sing leader spontaneously dictated in public!) Soon enough would sound forth perfect intervals in mixed meter with relentless percussive drive around a cantus firmus that the majority of those in attendance seemed perpetually starved of singing in daily life—a reality that would soon be well proven in the moment where it appeared that the roof would soon be raised. More generally, disparate histories would find common bond in remote locations of shared significance and in mutual acquaintances of contrastive contexts and periods of time, and various outlooks on life would be complimented and strengthened—if not also significantly challenged—by an insatiable zest for life in this creation and all the possibilities that it can and does afford. Any fear would be met by a dominant joy. Every day would be, to some degree and in some way, an exercise in the certainty to which all of us are approximate. And to put it rather simply, all of us are infinitely better on account of it.

It is this convergence of sorts that God has used to make us who we currently are: heralds with a charge unlike any other unto a certainty unlike any other, and thus catalysts unto action among a people of God's own making, and thus recipients of one God-sized marvel and surprised after another—no matter where in the world we are. Those in (and even throughout) the world whom we serve have none other than God to thank for being able themselves to participate in this grand convergence, this "shoulder-rubbing," in which Charles has played a significant role. And we—who carry on in our current diverse trajectories and surreal scenarios with our own thanksgiving for Charles and his contribution to our learning and careers and very lives—do so with that incarnational certainty to which we are ever approximate, in which we ever stand, out of which we pursue action in this world in ways that can truly only astonish us.

Notes

1 This and the subsequent texts from Colossians and Luke are the set of pericopal readings assigned for the commemoration of Johann Sebastian Bach, Georg Friedrich Handel, and Henry Purcell, as provisionally adopted by the 2009 General Convention of The Episcopal Church. The presented texts are personal translations from the original languages.

2 The modern English transliteration of the tetragrammaton "YHWH" is used primarily as an attempt to bring the modern English reader closer, by means of encounter, to the presentation of the divine name in the original Hebrew text. It is well known to this author that, in the attempt to resonate with the long-standing Christian and Jewish practices of deliberately avoiding oral articulation of the divine name, many Christian traditions endeavor to replicate such practice in print by substituting Greek- ("Kyrie") or Latin-equivalent ("Lord") translations for the tetragrammaton. Such practice, however, while also common in this author's own Christian confessional tradition, is by no means the exclusive translational practice in scriptural and liturgical-textual rendering, either in the author's Christian confession-

al tradition or in many others. Further, it is the intent of the author to not only take advantage of but also to advance his own Christian confessional tradition in the acknowledgment that (a) the divine name is revealed by God for actual use among God's own people in Christ Jesus; and (b) through the atoning work of Jesus Christ in his Passion, suffering, and death, the people of God indeed have full access to God, including in particular his divine name. While perhaps well-intentioned, the volitional Verbot ["prohibition"] of universal substitution for the tetragrammaton truly neither exemplifies a proper use of the divine name nor discourages its misuse. It rather simply accords with, reinforces, and advances a form of long-standing ecclesiastical piety that, while perhaps useful in certain circumstances, is by no means either necessary or particularly helpful in all circumstances, particularly that of scholarship.

3 Heb. *al-mishmerotham*, a prepositional phrase signifying, in a cultic context involving priests and Levites, the aspect and reality of a ceremonial office, function, or charge. See Francis Brown, S. R. Driver, and Charles A. Briggs, *The Brown-Driver-Briggs Hebrew and English Lexicon* (New York: Houghton, Miflin, 1906; reprinted, Peabody, MA: Hendrickson, 2005), mishmereth, 1038, 4. a.

4 Heb. *bicli-shir*, a prepositional construct form specifically denoting the instrumental accompaniment of song, distinct from the simpler *shir*, broadly denoting song in various forms, such as cultic or noncultic, accompanied or unaccompanied. Ibid., *shir*, 1010, 3.

5 Heb. *lehodoth*, a prepositional phrase referring to a "sacrifice of thanksgiving." Given that the dedicatory burnt offering does not directly correspond to one of the pre-existing prescripted levitical offerings but is, rather, especially occasional in nature, *lehodoth* is best rendered along the conceptual line of "thanksgiving in songs of liturgical worship." Ibid., *thodah*, 392, 2. In addition to the fact that such rendering accords better with the immediately proximate details articulated in verse 6, along with the immediate contextual account of the pericope, confirmation of this specific rendering is given through the Septuagint's use of *exomologeisthai* ("to praise") over and against possible alternatives that render the concept of tangible ritual sacrifice possible.

6 Heb. *machzezirim*, from *chazozirah*, quite likely an onomatopoeia for "to shatter." See E. Werner, "Musical Instruments," in George Arthur Buttrick, ed., *The Interpreter's Dictionary of the Bible*, vol. 3 (New York: Abingdon Press, 1962), 472, d.

7 Cf. 1 Chr. 23:5, 25:1.

8 Cf. 2 Chr. 29:25.

9 Cf. 2 Chr. 8:14.

10 2 Chr. 7:6 in the Septuagint.

11 Cf. Lev. 1:1–17.

12 Cf. 1 Chr. 25:3, 6.

13 An instrumental use of the preposition beth is indeed most likely in such context.

14 1 Chr. 25:1–3, personal translation from the Hebrew.

15 Cf.. *A Greek-English Lexicon of the New Testament and Other Early Christian Literature*, 3rd ed., rev. and edited Frederick William Danker (Chicago: University of Chicago Press, 2000), apophtheggomai, 125.

16 Eph. 5:2, personal translation.

17 Cf. 1 Pet. 1:4–10.

18 Cf. Heb. 5:5–9.

19 Dietrich Bartel, *Musica Poetica: Musical-Rhetorical Figures in German Baroque Music* (Lincoln: University of Nebraska Press, 1997), 65–66.

20 Ibid., 74–75.

21 Ibid., 75–77, 93–95, 106–111, 136–143.

22 Luke 1:1–4, personal translation.

23 Luke 3:1–6; cf. Matt. 3:1–6, Mark 1:2–6, and John 1:19–23.

24 Luke 3:15–18; cf. Matt. 3:11–12, Mark 1:7–8, and John 1:24–28.

25 Luke 3:21–22; cf. Matt. 3:13–17, Mark 1:9–11, and John 1:29–34.

26 Luke 3:23–38; cf. Matt. 1:1–17.

27 Luke 2:39–40; cf. Matt. 2:22–23.

28 Luke 3:7–9; cf. Matt. 3:7–10.

29 Luke 3:19–20; cf. Matt. 14:3–4 and Mark 6:17–18.

30 Luke 4:1–13; cf. Matt. 4:1–11 and Mark 1:12–13.

31 Luke 1:5–25.

32 Luke 1:26–38.

33 Luke 1:39–56.

34 Luke 1:57–80.

35 Luke 2:1–7. While Matthew indeed gives a narrative concerning the birth of Christ, as the text stands, he essentially narrates "around" the event, whereas Luke, albeit in ever-so-brief fashion, narrates the actual event itself.

36 Luke 2:8–20.

37 Luke 2:21–38.

38 Tertullian, "The Resurrection of the Flesh" 8.2, http://www.vatican.va/spirit/documents/spirit_20000908_tertulliano_en.html.

39 Cf. Luke 2:18.

Catalog of the Compositions of Charles W. Ore

Originally Compiled May 2006 and Updated June 2016 by Irene Beethe

Dates indicate year of publication or composition.

OWC 1   "Scattered by Sin"
For Unison Choir and Keyboard
1970 – Organ Works Corporation

11 Compositions for Organ, set 1
Dedication: The entire collection is dedicated to my parents.
1971 – CPH

     OWC 2   "All Glory Be to God Alone"
              Tune Name: ALL EHR UND LOB
     Dedication: For Ted Beck

     OWC 3   "All Glory Be to God on High"
              Tune Name: ALLEIN GOTT IN DER HÖH SEI EHR
              Dedication: For Connie

     OWC 4   "Arise and Shine in Splendor"
              Tune Name: O WELT, ICH MUSS DICH LASSEN

     OWC 5   "Lord, Keep Us Steadfast in Thy Word"
              Tune Name: ERHALT UNS, HERR, BEI DEINEM WORT

Notes: Each work has been assigned an OWC number by the compiler. This designation does not refer to Organ Works Corporation.

Comments on works are by the composer. Compiler's additions are in brackets.

Publishers include Concordia Publishing House (CPH); Augsburg Fortress (AF); MorningStar Music Publishers (MSM); and Organ Works Corporation. Pieces published by the latter may be obtained from 2523 Bluff Road, Seward, NE, 68434, or from Concordia University Nebraska Archives, 800 North Columbia, Seward, NE, 68434.

If no publisher is listed, the piece is in manuscript only.

OWC 6 "Oh, That I Had a Thousand Voices"
Tune Name: O DASS ICH TAUSEND (DRETZEL)
Dedication: For Heidi

OWC 7 "O Splendor of God's Glory Bright"
Tune Name: O HEILIGE DREIFALTIGKEIT
Dedication: For Janna

OWC 8 "To Shepherds as They Watched by Night"
Tune Name: PUER NOBIS NASCITUR

OWC 9 "Savior of the Nations, Come"
Tune Name: NUN KOMM, DER HEIDEN HEILAND

OWC 10 "Soul, Adorn Thyself with Gladness"
Tune Name: SCHMÜCKE DICH

OWC 11 "When All Thy Mercies, O My God"
Tune Name: WINCHESTER OLD

OWC 12 "Ye Watchers and Ye Holy Ones"
Tune Name: LASST UNS ERFREUEN

OWC 13 "Psalm 47"
For Unison Voices
1971 – Organ Works Corporation

Lisbon Psalms for Solo Voice and Piano, set 1
1975 – CPH

OWC 14 "Psalm 1"
Dedication: For Janna

OWC 15 "Psalm 4"
Dedication: For John-Paul

OWC 16 "Psalm 23"
Dedication: For Heidi

OWC 17 "Psalm 25"
Dedication: For Connie

Lisbon Psalms for Solo Voice and Organ, set 2
1975 – CPH

OWC 18 "Psalm 1"
Dedication: For Janna

OWC 19 "Psalm 4"
Dedication: For John-Paul

OWC 20 "Psalm 23"
Dedication: For Heidi

OWC 21 "Psalm 25"
        Dedication: For Connie

Lisbon Psalms for Choir
  1975

OWC 22 "Psalm 1"
        Dedication: For Janna

OWC 23 "Psalm 4"
        Dedication: For John-Paul

OWC 24 "Psalm 23"
        Dedication: For Heidi

OWC 25 "Psalm 25"
        Dedication: For Connie

OWC 26 A Festive Prelude on "Come Holy Ghost"
        Tune Name: KOMM, HEILIGER GEIST, HERRE GOTT
        For Organ
        Dedicated to J. W. and Anna Barbara Werling
        1975 – CPH

OWC 27 "Magnificat"
        For Solo Voice
        Dedication: For David and Connie at the time of marriage
        1975 – Organ Works Corporation

11 Compositions for Organ, set 2
  1976 – CPH

OWC 28 "Angels We Have Heard on High"
        Tune Name: GLORIA
        Dedication: For Paula Haar

OWC 29 "At the Lamb's High Feast"
        Tune Name: SONNE DER GERECHTIGKEIT
        Dedication: For Harlan McConnell
        Also found in *Augsburg Organ Library: Reformation*
        2016 – AF

OWC 30 "For All the Saints"
        Tune Name: SINE NOMINE
        Dedication: In memory of Rev. C. R. Zehnder

OWC 31 "I Come, O Savior, to Thy Table"
        Tune Name: ICH STERBE TÄGLICH

OWC 32 "In Thee Is Gladness"
        Tune Name: IN DIR IST FREUDE
        Dedication: In memory of Barrett Spach

OWC 33   "May God Bestow on Us His Grace"
           Tune Name: Es WOLL' GOTT UNS GENÄDIG SEIN

OWC 34   "Now"
           Tune Name: NOW
           Also found in *Augsburg Organ Library: Summer
           2004* – AF

OWC 35   "Now Let Us Pray to God the Holy Ghost"
           Tune Name: NUN BITTEN WIR

OWC 36   "Thy Strong Word Did Cleave the Darkness"
           Tune Name: EBENEZER

OWC 37   "With High Delight"
           Tune Name: MIT FREUDEN ZART
           Dedication: For Pauline Wente

OWC 38   "What Child Is This"
           Tune Name: GREENSLEEVES

OWC 39   "He Lives Forevermore"
           For Treble Voices and Instruments
           1976 – AF

OWC 40   Sonata 1
           For Organ
           Commissioned by CPH for the *Music for a Sunday Morning*
           series (vol. 4)
           1977 – CPH

OWC 41   "Open Our Hearts and Minds, O Lord"
           For Unison Choir and Keyboard
           1977 – Organ Works Corporation

OWC 42   Sonata 2
           For Organ

           Dedication: Sonata No. 2 was written during July of 1976, the month of Celebrating the Bicentennial of the American Revolution, and is dedicated to the memory of those early pioneers that chose to live on the Great Plains, especially my native state of Kansas.

           Commissioned by CPH for the *Music for a Sunday Morning* series (vol. 8)
           1978 – CPH

Hymn Preludes and Free Accompaniments, set 7
    For Organ
    1978 – AF

OWC 43 Tune Name: ALL SAINTS' NEW

OWC 44 Tune Name: CHESTERFIELD

OWC 45 Tune Name: CHRISTMAS DAWN

OWC 46 Tune Name: EIN LÄMMLEIN GEHT

OWC 47 Tune Name: ERSCHIENEN IST DER HERRLICH TAG

OWC 48 Tune Name: FORTUNATUS

OWC 49 Tune Name: HANOVER

OWC 50 Tune Name: HERZLIEBSTER JESU

OWC 51 Tune Name: ICH DANK' LIEBE HERRE

OWC 52 Tune Name: LOBE DEN HERREN

OWC 53 Tune Name: NATIONAL ANTHEM

OWC 54 Tune Name: NUN DANKET ALLE GOTT

OWC 55 "O Little Town of Bethlehem"
Tune Name: ST. LOUIS
For Organ
1979 – Organ Works Corporation

OWC 56 "O Lord, We Praise You"
Tune Name: GOTT SEI GELOBET UND GEBENEDEIET
For Organ
Written for *Hymn Preludes for Holy Communion*, vol. 2
1979 – CPH

OWC 57 "Gloria in Excelsis Deo"
A Festival Setting for SATB Choir and Keyboard
1980s – Organ Works Corporation

OWC 58 "Glory to God"
A Festival Setting for SATB Choir, Brass, Timpani, and
Keyboard
1980s – Organ Works Corporation

OWC 59 "Hail Thee, Festival Day"
Tune Name: SALVE FESTA DIES
For Instrumental Descant
1980s – Organ Works Corporation

OWC 60 "I Bind unto Myself"
Tune Name: ST. PATRICK'S BREASTPLATE
For Instrumental Descant
1980s – Organ Works Corporation

OWC 61   "The Church's One Foundation"
Tune Name: AURELIA
For Organ
1980s – Organ Works Corporation

OWC 62   "Let All Things Now Living"
Tune Name: THE ASH GROVE
For Organ
1980s – Organ Works Corporation

OWC 63   "At the Lamb's High Feast We Sing"
Tune Name: SONNE DER GERECHTIGKEIT
For Organ
1980s – Organ Works Corporation

OWC 64   "At the Name of Jesus" (unfinished)
Tune Name: KING'S WESTON
For Organ
1980 – Organ Works Corporation

OWC 65   "Sleep Little Babe"
A Setting for Keyboard and Descant Instrument
1980 – Organ Works Corporation

OWC 66   "Be Still, My Soul"
Tune Name: FINLANDIA
A Hymn Concertato for SATB Choir, Congregation,
Instruments (violin, flute, recorder, oboe, trumpet), and
Organ
1980 – Organ Works Corporation

OWC 67   "Glories of Your Name Are Spoken"
Tune Name: AUSTRIA
For Organ
1980 – Organ Works Corporation

OWC 68   "Beloved I Adore You"
For Two-part (S/B) Choir or Duet and Keyboard
1980 – Organ Works Corporation

OWC 69   "Savior of the Nations Come"
Tune Name: NUN KOMM, DER HEIDEN HEILAND
A Hymn Concertato for SATB Choir, Congregation,
Brass, and Organ
1980 – Organ Works Corporation

OWC 70   "Oh, Sing for Joy"
For Unison Choir, Percussion, and Organ
1980 – Organ Works Corporation

Eight Fanfares and Intradas
For Organ
These festive pieces may be used in a variety of ways. They work well as wedding fanfares and Gospel processions. For added flexibility, several of the pieces have been written so that the organist may begin playing at A, B, or C, depending on the length of piece desired.
1981 – AF

OWC 71   Fanfare in C Major
         Double Fanfare for Daily Living

OWC 72   Fanfare in D Major
         Freedom Fanfare in Non-metered Notation

OWC 73   Fanfare in E-flat Major
         Ceremonial Fanfare for Events Happening and Those Yet to Come

OWC 74   Intrada in E Major
         Intrada for an Occasion of Some Magnitude

OWC 75   Intrada in F Major
         Solemn Intrada for Concerns of a Serious Nature

OWC 76   Intrada in G Major
         An Intrada for All Saints and Seasons

OWC 77   Fanfare in A-flat Major
         Fanfare for Reeds and Other Festal Stops

OWC 78   Fanfare in B-flat Major
         Fanfare for the Baroque Spirit

OWC 79   "Oh, Come, All Ye Faithful"
         Tune Name: ADESTE FIDELES
         Text: Constance L. Ore
         A Festival Processional for Congregation, Choirs, and Instruments
         1981 – AF

OWC 80   "O Come, Lord Jesus"
         For Unison Choir and Keyboard
         1981 – Organ Works Corporation

OWC 81   Four Fanfares
         For Three Trumpets
         1981 – Organ Works Corporation

OWC 82   "Psalm 31"
         For SATB Choir, Congregation, and Organ
         1981 – Organ Works Corporation

OWC 83 "Dungeons and Dragons"
For Solo Piano
Dedication: For John-Paul
1981 – Organ Works Corporation

OWC 84 "Tobogganing"
For Solo Piano
Dedication: For John-Paul
1981 – Organ Works Corporation

OWC 85 "Pacific Hills Anniversary Hymn"
Text: Duane Fieck
A Hymn for the Congregation
Written for the 25th anniversary of Pacific Hills Lutheran
Church, Omaha, Nebraska
1981

OWC 86 "O Come, Lord Jesus, Come"
An Advent Response for Unison Choir and Congregation
Dedication: For the Pacific Hills Choir
1981 – Organ Works Corporation

11 Compositions for Organ, set 3
1982 – CPH

OWC 87 "Battle Hymn of the Republic"
Tune Name: BATTLE HYMN

OWC 88 "Beautiful Savior"
Tune Name: SCHÖNSTER HERR JESU
Dedication: For Connie

OWC 89 "Dearest Jesus, We Are Here"
Tune Name: LIEBSTER JESU, WIR SIND HIER
Dedication: For the baptism of Elizabeth Bea Wake

OWC 90 "Glory Be to Jesus"
Tune Name: WEM IN LEIDENSTAGEN
Dedication: For Willis Mundt

OWC 91 "I Know that My Redeemer Lives"
Tune Name: DUKE STREET

OWC 92 "It Happened on That Fateful Night"
Tune Name: BOURBON

OWC 93 "Lift High the Cross"
Tune Name: CRUCIFER

OWC 94　"Salvation unto Us Has Come"
Tune Name: Es ist das Heil
Dedication: For Barry and Donna Bobb
Also found in *Augsburg Organ Library: Reformation*
2016 – AF

OWC 95　"The Church's One Foundation"
Tune Name: Aurelia

OWC 96　"The First Noel"
Tune Name: The First Noel

OWC 97　"Welcome, Happy Morning"
Tune Name: Fortunatus

OWC 98　"Psalm 96"
For SATB Choir, Timpani, and Brass
1982 – Organ Works Corporation

OWC 99　"Psalm 117"
For Unison Voices and Keyboard
1982 – Organ Works Corporation

OWC 100　"Father, the Time Has Come"
A Cantata in Five Parts for SATB Choir, Three Soloists,
Four-part Brass, Keyboard, and Congregation
Requested by David Held for Concordia Singers, Fall 1981
1982 – Organ Works Corporation

OWC 101　Sing We, Now Rejoice"
(alternate title: "Ring, Bells, Ring")
Tune Name: In dulci jubilo
A Festival Processional for Congregation, Choirs, and
Instruments (violin, flute, recorder, oboe, trumpet, and organ)
1983 – AF

OWC 102　"At the Lamb's High Feast We Sing"
Tune Name: Sonne der Gerechtigkeit
A Hymn Concertato for SATB Choir, Congregation,
Instruments, and Organ
1983 – Organ Works Corporation

OWC 103　"Brother James' Air/The Ash Grove"
Tune Names: Brother James' Air and The Ash Grove
A Hymn Concertato for SATB Choir, Congregation, Flute,
Brass, and Organ
1984 – Organ Works Corporation

OWC 104 "The King of Glory Comes"
Tune Name: THE KING OF GLORY
A Hymn Concertato for SATB Choir, Diverse Instruments,
Keyboard, and Congregation
1987 – Organ Works Corporation

OWC 105 "Given for Me"
A Worship Service Written for Congregation, Service
Leader, Optional Brass/Woodwinds, and Keyboard
1988 – Organ Works Corporation

OWC 106 "The Hand of the Lord"
A Setting of Ezekiel 37:1–14 for SATB Choir
1988 – Organ Works Corporation

11 Compositions for Organ, set 4
1989 – CPH

OWC 107 "Ah, Holy Jesus, How Hast Thou Offended"
(alternate title: "O Dearest Jesus, What Law Have You
Broken")
Tune Name: HERZLIEBSTER JESU
Dedication: For Janna Christian

OWC 108 "Angels We Have Heard on High"
Tune Name: GLORIA
Dedication: For Judy and the choir at Pacific Hills
Lutheran Church, Omaha, Nebraska

OWC 109 "At the Lamb's High Feast We Sing"
Tune Name: SONNE DER GERECHTIGKEIT
Dedication: For David Held and the Concordia
Singers

OWC 110 "Behold a Host Arrayed in White"
Tune Name: DEN STORE HVIDE FLOK
Commissioned by Salem Lutheran Church of Rosehill,
Tomball, Texas

OWC 111 "Christ Be My Leader"
Tune Name: SLANE
Dedication: For David Haar

OWC 112 "Earth and All Stars"
Tune Name: EARTH AND ALL STARS
Dedication: For John-Paul

OWC 113 "Go Tell It on the Mountain"
Tune Name: GO TELL IT
Dedication: For Heidi and Jon

OWC 114   "Once He Came in Blessing"
Tune Name: Gottes Sohn ist kommen
Dedication: For John and Isabell

OWC 115   "Savior of the Nations, Come"
Tune Name: Nun komm, der Heiden Heiland
Dedication: For Connie, Heidi, Janna, and John-Paul

OWC 116   "The First Day of the Week"
Tune Name: Kentucky 93rd
Dedication: For Connie

OWC 117   "The Lord's My Shepherd, Leading Me"
Tune Name: Brother James' Air
Dedication: For Merle Radke

OWC 118   "Praise and Thanksgiving"
Tune Name: Bunessan
For Instrumental Descant
1990s – Organ Works Corporation

OWC 119   "Let All Mortal Flesh Keep Silence"
Tune Name: Picardy
For Instrumental Descant
1990s – Organ Works Corporation

OWC 120   "My Hope Is Built on Nothing Less"
Tune Name: Melita
For Instrumental Descant
1990s – Organ Works Corporation

OWC 121   "Lord, Enthroned in Heavenly Splendor"
Tune Name: Bryn Calfaria
For Instrumental Descant
1990s – Organ Works Corporation

OWC 122   "Crown Him with Many Crowns"
Tune Name: Diademata
A Hymn Concertato for SATB Choir, Congregation,
Brass, and Organ
1990 – Organ Works Corporation

OWC 123   "Omnes Learned Doctora"
Text: Students and faculty at St. John Lutheran School
For Unison Choir and Keyboard
Dedication: For St. John School
1990 – Organ Works Corporation

OWC 124   "A Mighty Fortress"
           Tune Name: EIN FESTE BURG
           For Organ
           Dedication: In memory of Rev. C. R. Zehnder
           1990 – CPH

OWC 125   "All Glory Be to God on High"
           Tune Name: ALLEIN GOTT IN DER HÖH
           For Instrumental Descant
           1990 – Organ Works Corporation

OWC 126   "Built on a Rock the Church Shall Stand"
           Tune Name: KIRKEN DEN ER ET GAMMELT HUS
           For Instrumental Descant
           1990 – Organ Works Corporation

OWC 127   "My Crown of Creation"
           Tune Name: SIMPLE GIFTS
           An Anthem Written for SATB Choir and Organ
           Originally written in 1987 as "The Lord of the Dance"
           1991 – MSM

11 Compositions for Organ, set 5
    1991 – CPH

    OWC 128   "Cold December Flies Away"
               Tune Name: LO DESEMBRE CONGELAT
               Dedication: For Carol Schroeder-McDaniel

    OWC 129   "I Am Jesus' Little Lamb"
               Tune Name: WEIL ICH JESU SCHÄFLEIN BIN
               Dedication: In memory of Erika Steiner (1975–1981)

    OWC 130   "I Love to Tell the Story"
               Tune Name: HANKEY
               Dedication: For Nathan and Betty Wadewitz

    OWC 131   "Jesus Has Come and Brings Pleasure"
               Tune Name: JESUS IST KOMMEN, GRUND EWIGER FREUDE
               Dedication: For Barbara Wahlert

    OWC 132   "Jesus, I Will Ponder Now"
               Tune Name: JESU, KREUZ, LEIDEN UND PEIN
               Dedication: For Erna Werling-Wilson

    OWC 133   "Jesus, Priceless Treasure"
               Tune Name: JESU, MEINE FREUDE
               Dedication: For Lee Werling

OWC 134   "Joy to the World"
               Tune Name: ANTIOCH
               Dedication: For Hans and Agnes Schau
               Originally written for trumpet and organ

OWC 135   "Lord Jesus, Think on Me"
               (alternate title: "Not All the Blood of Beasts")
               Tune Name: SOUTHWELL
               Dedication: For Adelaide Werling-Sterz

OWC 136   "Lord of Glory, You Have Bought Us"
               (alternate title: "Love Divine, All Loves Excelling")
               Tune Name: HYFRYDOL
               Dedication: For Walter and Bernice Werling-Krumm

OWC 137   "Prepare the Royal Highway"
               Tune Name: BEREDEN VÄG FÖR HERRAN
               Dedication: For Scott Weidler

OWC 138   "Sent Forth by God's Blessing"
               Tune Name: THE ASH GROVE
               Dedication: For Jim Oschwald

Hymn Descants for Treble Instruments
1992 – AF

OWC 139   "Oh, Come, All Ye Faithful"
               Tune Name: ADESTE FIDELES

OWC 140   "Prepare the Royal Highway"
               Tune Name: BEREDEN VÄG FÖR HERRAN

OWC 141   "Lord Enthroned in Heavenly Splendor"
               Tune Name: BRYN CALFARIA

OWC 142   "Of the Father's Love Begotten"
               Tune Name: DIVINUM MYSTERIUM

OWC 143   "Earth and All Stars"
               Tune Name: EARTH AND ALL STARS
               Dedication: For Grant Peters

OWC 144   "A Mighty Fortress Is Our God"
               Tune Name: EIN FESTE BURG (rhythmic)
               Dedication: For Grant Peters

OWC 145   "Lo, How a Rose Is Growing"
               Tune Name: ES IST EIN ROS
               Dedication: For Kermit Peters

OWC 146   "Angels We Have Heard on High"
           Tune Name: GLORIA

OWC 147   "Go Tell It on the Mountain"
           Tune Name: GO TELL IT
           Dedication: For the students at Concordia College
           Nebraska

OWC 148   "Good Christian Friends, Rejoice" (two arrangements)
           Tune Name: IN DULCI JUBILO
           Dedications: #1—For Heidi Rath-Hope
                        #2—For the students of St. John School,
                                 Seward, Nebraska

OWC 149   "Jesus Has Come and Brings Pleasure"
           Tune Name: JESUS IST KOMMEN, GRUND EWIGER FREUDE

OWC 150   "The First Day of the Week"
           Tune Name: KENTUCKY 93RD
           Dedication: For Constance Ore

OWC 151   "Now All the Vault of Heaven Resounds"
           Tune Name: LASST UNS ERFREUEN
           Dedication: For Andrew Schultz

OWC 152   "Savior of the Nations, Come"
           Tune Name: NUN KOMM, DER HEIDEN HEILAND

OWC 153   "Beautiful Savior"
           Tune Name: SCHÖNSTER HERR JESU
           Dedication: For Sue Baade

OWC 154A   "The Seventh Trumpet"
           For Solo Organ
           1994 – Organ Works Corporation

OWC 154B   "The Seventh Trumpet"
           For Organ and Trumpet
           1994 – Organ Works Corporation
           Reworked for solo trumpet
           2003

OWC 155   "Concordia, Concordia!"
           For Unison Choir and Keyboard
           Dedication: For the seventh grade class at St. John
           Lutheran School, Seward, Nebraska
           Requested by an anonymous person
           1993 – Organ Works Corporation

OWC 156   "Our God, Our Help in Ages Past"
           Tune Name: St. Anne
           A Hymn Alternation for SATB Choir, Descanting
           Instrument, Congregation, and Keyboard
           1994 – CPH

OWC 157   "Rejoice, O Pilgrim Throng"
           Tune Name: Marion
           A Hymn Concertato for SATB Choir, Brass, Congregation,
           and Organ
           1994 – CPH

OWC 158   "Silent Night, Holy Night"
           Tune Name: Stille Nacht
           For Organ and Oboe (or treble instrument)
           Dedication: For Kermit Peters
           1994 – CPH

OWC 159   "The King Shall Come"
           Tune Name: Consolation
           For Instrumental Descant
           1994 – Organ Works Corporation

OWC 160   "Immortal, Invisible, God Only Wise"
           Tune Name: St. Denio
           For Instrumental Descant
           1994 – Organ Works Corporation

11 Compositions for Organ, set 6
     1995 – CPH

    OWC 161   "Away in a Manger"
               Tune Name: Away in a Manger

    OWC 162   "Away in a Manger"
               Tune Name: Cradle Song
               Dedication: For Jon, Sue, and Catherine Grace

    OWC 163   "Away in a Manger"
               Tune Name: Cradle Song
               Dedication: For John Eggert

    OWC 164   "Come, O Long-Expected Jesus"
               Tune Name: Jefferson
               Dedication: For David Polley

    OWC 165   "Hark! The Herald Angels Sing"
               Tune Name: Mendelssohn
               Dedication: In memory of Martha Wake

OWC 166   "Let All Together Praise Our God"
Tune Name: LOBT GOTT, IHR CHRISTEN
Dedication: For Connie

OWC 167   "Lo, How a Rose Is Growing"
Tune Name: ES IST EIN ROS
Dedication: For Kermit Peters
Originally written for organ and oboe

OWC 168   "Of the Father's Love Begotten"
Tune Name: DIVINUM MYSTERIUM
Dedication: For Steve Hoelter

OWC 169   "Oh Come, Oh Come, Emmanuel"
Tune Name: VENI, EMMANUEL
Dedication: For John Horak

OWC 170   "O Morning Star, How Fair and Bright"
Tune Name: WIE SCHÖN LEUCHTET
Dedication: To Martin W. Raabe

OWC 171   "The King Shall Come"
Tune Name: CONSOLATION
Dedication: For Irene Beethe

OWC 172   "Who Can Conceive the One True God"
Text: Jaroslav J. Vajda
A Hymn Concertato for SATB Choir, Congregation,
Brass, and Organ
1995 – Organ Works Corporation

OWC 173   "O Morning Star, How Fair and Bright"
Tune Name: WIE SCHÖN LEUCHTET
A Hymn Concertato for SATB Choir, Brass, Solo Trumpet
or Oboe, Congregation, and Organ
1996 – CPH

OWC 174   "O God of God, O Light of Light"
Tune Name: O GROSSER GOTT
A Hymn Concertato for SATB Choir, Congregation,
Brass, and Organ
1996 – CPH

OWC 175   "There Is a Green Hill Far Away"
An Anthem for SATB Choir, Congregation, Claves,
Handbells, Optional Flute, and Organ
1996 – CPH

OWC 176   "This Is My Son"
           An Anthem for SATB Choir, Congregation, Trumpet, and
           Organ
           Dedication: Written for First Presbyterian Church,
           Atlanta, Georgia
           1996 – CPH

OWC 177   "O Day Full of Grace"
           Tune Name: DEN SIGNEDE DAG
           A Hymn Concertato for SATB Choir, Congregation,
           Brass, and Organ
           1996 – Organ Works Corporation

OWC 178   "Gaze in Amazement"
           Text: Jaroslav J. Vajda
           A Hymn Concertato for SATB Choir, Congregation,
           Brass, and Organ
           Written for the 110th Anniversary of Trinity Lutheran
           Church, Cedar Rapids, Iowa
           1996 – Organ Works Corporation

OWC 179   "Winter Night Gives Birth to Day"
           A Hymn for Congregation and Choir
           1996 – Organ Works Corporation

OWC 180   "A Time and a Purpose"
           An Anthem for SATB Choir, Congregation, and Organ
           1998 – CPH

OWC 181   "Praise God in His Temple"
           Tune Name: OLD HUNDREDTH
           An Anthem for SATB Choir, Congregation, Brass, and
           Organ
           2000 – Organ Works Corporation

Eight
    For Organ
    A collection that highlights the various tonal capabilities of the
    organ
    Commissioned by the Oklahoma City AGO Chapter
    2000 – CPH

    OWC 182   Entrance

    OWC 183   Flight

    OWC 184   Diversion 1

    OWC 185   Procession 1

OWC 186   Excursion

OWC 187   Procession 2

OWC 188   Diversion 2

OWC 189   Exit

OWC 190   "Jesus on the Mountain Peak"
Tune Name: SEWARD
Written for *Hymnal Supplement 98: Organ Prelude Edition*, vol. 1
2000 – CPH

OWC 191   "Rejoice, Rejoice, Believers"
Tune Name: HAF TRONES LAMPA FÄRDIG
Written for *Hymnal Supplement 98: Organ Prelude Edition*, vol. 1
2000 – CPH

OWC 192   "In Silent Pain the Eternal Son"
Tune Name: REALITY
Written for *Hymnal Supplement 98: Organ Prelude Edition*, vol. 2
2000 – CPH

OWC 193   "Christ Is Risen, Christ Is Living"
Tune Name: CENTRAL (ARGENTINA)
Written for *Hymnal Supplement 98: Organ Prelude Edition*, vol. 2
2000 – CPH

OWC 194   "Now Is Eternal Life"
Tune Name: CHRISTCHURCH
Written for *Hymnal Supplement 98: Organ Prelude Edition*, vol. 2
2000 – CPH

OWC 195   "We Know that Christ Is Raised"
Tune Name: ENGELBERG
Written for *Hymnal Supplement 98: Organ Prelude Edition*, vol. 3
2001 – CPH

OWC 196   "The Infant Priest Was Holy Born"
Tune Name: ROCKINGHAM OLD
Written for *Hymnal Supplement 98: Organ Prelude Edition*, vol. 3
2001 – CPH

11 Compositions for Organ, set 7
2002 – CPH

OWC 197   "Amazing Grace, How Sweet the Sound"
Tune Name: NEW BRITAIN

OWC 198   "Crown Him with Many Crowns"
Tune Name: DIADEMATA

OWC 199   "When in Our Music God Is Glorified"
Tune Name: ENGELBERG
Dedication: To Lutheran A Cappella Choir
of Milwaukee
Commissioned by Dr. and Mrs. William A. Raabe

OWC 200   "Praise Him"
Tune Name: HAL'LUHU

OWC 201   "Alleluia! Sing to Jesus"
Tune Name: HYFRYDOL
Dedication: Commissioned by Christ Lutheran
Church, Norfolk, Nebraska, in thanksgiving to God
for the 50 years of service of Margaret Sommerfeld as
a church organist

OWC 202   "O Day Full of Grace"
Tune Name: DEN SIGNEDE DAG
Dedication: To Nancy M. Raabe

OWC 203   "O God of God, O Light of Light"
Tune Name: O GROSSER GOTT

OWC 204   "Rejoice, O Pilgrim Throng"
Tune Name: MARION
Commissioned for the 125th Anniversary Year of
Jubilee, St. John Lutheran Church, Forest Park, Illinois

OWC 205   "Grant Us Peace"
Tune Name: SIM SHALOM
Dedication: For Paul Kastens

OWC 206   "The People of Israel Shall Keep the Sabbath"
Tune Name: V'SHAM'RU

OWC 207   "What a Friend We Have in Jesus"
Tune Name: CONVERSE

OWC 208   "When in Our Music God Is Glorified"
Tune Name: ENGELBERG
A Hymn Concertato for SATB Choir, Congregation, Brass,
and Organ
2002 – Organ Works Corporation

OWC 209   "Amazing Grace, How Sweet the Sound"
Tune Name: NEW BRITAIN
Written to go before "Amazing Grace" in vol. 7 of *11 Compositions for Organ* [OWC 197]
2002 – Organ Works Corporation

OWC 210   "Voices Raised to You"
Tune Name: SONG OF PRAISE
Written for *Hymnal Supplement 98: Organ Prelude Edition*, vol. 5
2003 – CPH

OWC 211   "All You Works of God, Bless the Lord!"
Tune Name: LINSTEAD
Written for *Hymnal Supplement 98: Organ Prelude Edition*, vol. 5
2003 – CPH

OWC 212   "The Lord Has Done Great Things Indeed"
Tune Name: REUNION
Text: Constance L. Ore based on Psalm 126:3
A Hymn Concertato for SATB Choir, Brass, Timpani, Congregation, and Organ
Written for the All-Choir Reunion at Concordia University Nebraska, 2004
2004 – Organ Works

OWC 213   "We Praise You and Acknowledge You, O God"
Tune Name: THAXTED
For Congregation, Organ, and Instruments
Dedication: Constance Louise Ore
2008 – CPH

11 Compositions for Organ, set 8
2008 – CPH

OWC 214   "Lord, Whose Love through Humble Service"
Tune Name: BEACH SPRING
Dedication: Commissioned by Bethel Lutheran Church, Dallas, Texas,
for Pastor Don Berg at the time of his retirement

OWC 215   "A Mighty Fortress"
Tune Name: EIN FESTE BURG
A revised version of the 1990 publication [OWC 124]

OWC 216   "How Firm a Foundation"
Tune Name: FOUNDATION

OWC 217   "Christ, the Word of God Incarnate"
          (alternate titles: "Faith and Truth and Life Bestowing,"
          "Gracious God, You Send Great Blessings)
          Tune Name: HOLY MANNA

OWC 218   "Alleluia! Sing to Jesus"
          Tune Name: HYFRYDOL
          Dedication: In thanksgiving to God for 50 years
          of service of Margaret Sommerfeld as church organist,
          Christ Lutheran Church, Norfolk, Nebraska

OWC 219   "No Tramp of Soldiers' Marching Feet"
          (alternate title: "Your Hand, O Lord, in Days of Old")
          Tune Name: KINGSFOLD

OWC 220   "Come, My Beloved"
          Tune Name: L'CHA DODI
          Dialogue for Krummhorn and Cornet
          Variations on a Hebrew Folksong

OWC 221   "Swiftly Pass the Clouds of Glory"
          Tune Name: LOVE'S LIGHT

OWC 222   Introduction to "Amazing Grace, How Sweet
          the Sound"
          Tune Name: NEW BRITAIN

OWC 223   "Silent Night, Holy Night"
          Tune Name: STILLE NACHT
          Arranged for solo organ from the 1994 publication for
          organ and oboe [OWC 158]
          Dedicated to Kermit Peters

OWC 224   "Draw Us in the Spirit's Tether"
          Tune Name: UNION SEMINARY
          Written at the request of Ben Baldus

OWC 225   "Glory Rock"
          Tune Name: TOPLADY
          For Organ
          Dedication: To Constance L. Ore
          2009

OWC 226   "Jesus on the Mountain Peak"
          Tune Name: SEWARD
          For Organ
          Dedicated to Greg Paul on the occasion of his
          25th anniversary in music ministry
          2009

OWC 227   "The Star-Spangled Banner"
Tune Name: NATIONAL ANTHEM
For Organ
A revised version is included in *11 Compositions for Organ*,
set 9 [OWC 259].
2009

OWC 228   "O Splendor of God's Glory Bright"
Tune Name: PUTNAM
A Hymn Concertato for SATB Choir, Descant, Instruments
or Handbells, Congregation, and Organ
Commissioned by Hope Lutheran Church,
Shawnee, Kansas
An organ version of the prelude is available in
11 Compositions for Organ, set 9 [OWC 257].
2010 – Organ Works Corporation

OWC 229   A Festive Prelude on "Come, Holy Ghost, God and Lord"
Tune Name: KOMM, HEILIGER GEIST, HERRE GOTT
For Organ
Dedicated to J. W. and Anna Barbara Werling
A revised version of a 1975 publication [OWC 26]
2010

OWC 230   "Just As I Am, without One Plea"
Tune Name: WOODWORTH
For Organ
Dedication: In memory of Arlo Henry Schroeder
(1929–2011)
A version is included in *11 Compositions for Organ*,
set 9 [OWC 255].
2010

OWC 230a "Just As I Am, without One Plea"
Tune Name: WOODWORTH
For Organ and E-flat Alto Sax or Treble Instrument in C
or B-flat
Dedication: In memory of Arlo Henry Schroeder (1929–2011)
This setting was commissioned by the family of Arlo Henry
Schroeder.
A version is included in *Three for Two* [OWC 243].
After 2010

OWC 231   "When in Our Music God Is Glorified"
Tune Name: ENGELBERG
For Organ
After 2010

OWC 232   "Glory Rock"
          Tune Name: Toplady
          For Organ
          Dedication: In loving memory of Constance L. Ore
          (1937–2010)
          "When I soar to worlds unknown—Glory Hallelujah"
          A revised version of a 2009 publication [OWC 225]
          After 2010

OWC 233   "In Silent Pain the Eternal Son"
          Tune Name: Reality
          For Organ
          After 2010

OWC 234   "The Infant Priest Was Holy Born"
          Tune Name: Rockingham Old
          For Organ
          After 2010

OWC 235   "Voices Raised to You"
          Tune Name: Song of Praise
          For Organ
          A revised version of a 2003 publication
          After 2010

OWC 236   "O Morning Star, How Fair and Bright"
          Tune Name: Wie Schön Leuchtet
          For Organ
          Dedicated to Martin W. Raabe
          After 2010

OWC 237   "Salvation unto Us Has Come"—Adagio and Fugue
          Tune Name: Es ist das Heil
          For Organ
          Commissioned by Barry and Donna Bobb, 1977
          The Adagio was published in *11 Compositions for Organ*,
          set 3 [OWC 94].
          The Fugue will be published in *11 Compositions for Organ*,
          set 10 [OWC 272].

OWC 238   "How Shall They Hear, Who Have Not Heard"
          Tune Name: Angelus (Du meiner Seelen)
          Written for *Hymnal Supplement 98: Organ Prelude Edition*,
          vol. 4
          2002 – CPH

OWC 239 "Weary of All Trumpeting," setting 2
Tune Name: DISTLER
Written for *Hymnal Supplement 98: Organ Prelude Edition*,
vol.4
2002 – CPH

OWC 240 "Amazing Grace, How Sweet the Sound"
Tune Name: NEW BRITAIN
Some portions, with revisions, will be published in
11 Compositions for Organ, set 10 [OWC 266, 267, and 268].
2008–14 (hymn, 2008; variation 1, 2013; variations 2
and 3, 2014; fugue, 2013–14)

OWC 241 "Now That the Daylight Fills the Sky"
For Organ
2013

Three for Two: Spiritual Expressions for Keyboard and Instrument
2013 – CPH

OWC 242 "Just a Closer Walk with Thee"
Tune Name: CLOSER WALK

OWC 243 "Just As I Am, without One Plea"
Tune Name: WOODWORTH
Dedication: In Memory of Arlo Henry Schroeder
(1929–2011)
A solo organ version is available in *11 Compositions
for Organ*, set 9 [OWC 255].

OWC 244 "What a Friend We Have in Jesus"
Tune Name: CONVERSE
A solo organ version is available in *11 Compositions
for Organ*, set 7 [OWC 207].

OWC 245 "Away in a Manger"
Tune Name: CRADLE SONG
For Organ
Written for *Hymn Prelude Library: Lutheran Service Book*,
vol. 2, Tunes BC
2013 – CPH

OWC 246 "Comfort, Comfort Ye My People"
(alternate title: "Praise to You and Adoration")
Tune Name: FREU DICH SEHR
For Organ
Written for *Hymn Prelude Library: Lutheran Service Book*,
vol. 4, Tunes FG
2013 – CPH

OWC 247　"Christ Church"
　　　　　For Organ
　　　　　New Arrangement
　　　　　2012

OWC 248　"God Separated Day from Night"
　　　　　For Organ and Congregation
　　　　　Text: Dick Weigman
　　　　　Four-verse Hymn
　　　　　After 2010

OWC 249　"Brightest and Best"
　　　　　Tune Name: MORNING STAR
　　　　　For Organ
　　　　　Written for *Hymn Prelude Library: Lutheran Service Book*,
　　　　　vol. 7, Tunes M
　　　　　2015 – CPH

11 Compositions for Organ, set 9
　2012 – CPH

　　OWC 250　A Festive Prelude on "Come, Holy Ghost,
　　　　　　　God and Lord"
　　　　　　　Tune Name: KOMM, HEILIGER GEIST, HERRE GOTT
　　　　　　　Dedication: J. W. and Anna Barbara Werling

　　OWC 251　"We Know that Christ Is Raised"
　　　　　　　(alternate titles: "When in Our Music God Is Glorified";
　　　　　　　"All Praise to Thee, for Thou, O King Divine")
　　　　　　　Tune Name: ENGELBERG

　　OWC 252　"Glory Rock"
　　　　　　　"When I Soar to Worlds Unknown—Glory, Hallelujah!"
　　　　　　　Tune Names: TOPLADY and BATTLE HYMN
　　　　　　　Dedication: In loving memory of Constance L. Ore
　　　　　　　(1937–2010)
　　　　　　　A second revision of the 2009 version [OWC 225]

　　OWC 253　"In Silent Pain the Eternal Son"
　　　　　　　Tune Name: REALITY

　　OWC 254　"Jesus on the Mountain Peak"
　　　　　　　Tune Name: SEWARD
　　　　　　　Dedication: To Greg Paul on the occasion of his
　　　　　　　25th anniversary in music ministry

　　OWC 255　"Just as I Am, without One Plea"
　　　　　　　Tune Name: WOODWORTH
　　　　　　　Dedication: In memory of Arlo Henry Schroeder
　　　　　　　(1929–2011)

OWC 256   "O Morning Star, How Fair and Bright"
          Tune Name: WIE SCHÖN LEUCHTET
          Dedication: To Martin W. Raabe

OWC 257   "O Savior of Our Fallen Race"
          (alternate title: "O Splendor of God's Glory Bright")
          Tune Name: PUTNAM
          Commissioned by Hope Lutheran Church,
          Shawnee, Kansas

OWC 258   "When I Survey the Wondrous Cross"
          (alternate title: "The Infant Priest Was Holy Born")
          Tune Name: ROCKINGHAM OLD

OWC 259   "The Star-Spangled Banner"
          Tune Name: STAR-SPANGLED BANNER

OWC 260 "Voices Raised to You We Offer"
          Tune Name: SONG OF PRAISE

OWC 261   "When I Survey the Wondrous Cross"
          (alternate title: "The Infant Priest Was Holy Born")
          Tune Name: ROCKINGHAM OLD
          For Organ
          Revision of 2001 version, which is available in
          11 Compositions for Organ, set 9 [OWC 258]
          2016

OWC 262   "I Am Trusting Thee, Lord Jesus"
          Tune Name: STEPHANOS
          For Organ
          2016

OWC 263   Variations on "Savior of the Nations, Come"
          Tune Name: NUN KOMM DER HEIDEN HEILAND
          For Organ
          2016

OWC 264   "Rise, Shine, You People"
          Tune Name: WOJTKIEWIECZ
          Hymn Concertato for SATB Choir, Congregation,
          Trumpet, and Organ
          Dedication: For Bill and Nancy Raabe
          2016

OWC 265   "Christ Is Made the Sure Foundation"
Tune Name: WESTMINSTER ABBEY
A Hymn Concertato for SATB Choir (optional quartet,
duet, or soloist), Congregation, Brass Quintet, Timpani,
and Organ
Dedication: Commissioned by Dr. William A. and Nancy
M. Raabe to honor the ministry of Rev. Dr. Franklin A.
Wilson at Luther Memorial   Church, Madison,
Wisconsin
Written in a style to honor Henry Purcell,
composer of the hymn tune
2016

11 Compositions for Organ, set 10
Forthcoming 2017 (CPH)

OWC 266   Prelude on "Amazing Grace"
Tune Name: NEW BRITAIN

OWC 267   Variation on "Amazing Grace"
Tune Name: NEW BRITAIN
"So God created humankind in his image."
(Genesis 1:26)

OWC 268   Fugue on "Amazing Grace"
Tune Name: NEW BRITAIN
"When the fullness of time had come, God sent his Son,
born of a woman, born under the law, in order to
redeem those who were under the Law, so that we
might receive adoption as children . . . and if a child
then also an heir, through God." (Galatians 4:4)

OWC 269   "Rejoice, Rejoice, Believers"
Tune Name: HAF TRONES LAMPA FÄRDIG
Written in 2000, manuals only; rewritten 2016

OWC 270   "O Day of Peace"
Tune Name: JERUSALEM
Written by Charles for himself—a great text at a
troubled time.

OWC 271   "Just a Closer Walk with Thee"
Tune Name: CLOSER WALK
This is a solo organ arrangement from a version in
Three for Two [OWC 242].

OWC 272   Fugue on "Salvation unto Us Has Come"
Tune Name: ES IST DAS HEIL
Dedication: For Barry and Donna Bobb
Written in 1977 and extensively revised in 2015
The Prelude written with this Fugue in 1977 is found
in *11 Compositions for Organ*, set 3 [OWC 94].

OWC 273   "I Am Trusting Thee, Lord Jesus"
Tune Name: STEPHANOS

OWC 274   "Christ Is Made the Sure Foundation"
(organ introduction)
Tune Name: WESTMINSTER ABBEY
Dedication: Commissioned by Dr. William A. and
Nancy M. Raabe to honor the ministry of Rev. Dr.
Franklin A. Wilson at Luther Memorial Church,
Madison, Wisconsin

OWC 275   "Christ Is Made the Sure Foundation"
(organ solo or hymn accompaniment)
Tune Name: WESTMINSTER ABBEY
Dedication: Commissioned by Dr. William A. and
Nancy M. Raabe to honor the ministry of Rev. Dr.
Franklin A. Wilson at Luther Memorial Church,
Madison, Wisconsin

OWC 276   "Rise, Shine, You People"
Tune Name: WOJTKIEWIECZ
Commissioned by Bill and Nancy Raabe

Contributors

Christopher S. Ahlman is a career missionary through The Lutheran Church—Missouri Synod (LCMS) in Leipzig, Germany. In this role Christopher serves as assistant pastor for a new church plant of the Independent Evangelical Lutheran Church—the partner church body of the LCMS in Germany. He works with LCMS area facilitators and mission partners in developing materials that witness through music and strengthen the LCMS regional strategy to expand existing Lutheran communities and establish new churches. He also assists the regional director of Eurasia in the development, implementation, and evaluation of a strategy for planting new churches in the urban European context.

Irene Beethe serves as Kantor at Zion Lutheran Church in Wausau, WI. She studied with Charles Ore as an undergraduate student at Concordia in Seward, NE. She has served in a variety of musical capacities in schools and congregations in Michigan and Wisconsin. While pursuing her master's in church music degree at Concordia in Mequon, WI, she spent countless hours visiting with Charles and Connie about Charles' life and growth as a musician, which led to her writing his biography. This Festschrift is a portion of that document. It is a great honor to present this volume to him.

Jeffrey Blersch is associate professor of music and university organist at Concordia University Nebraska, where he teaches studio organ as well as courses in organ improvisation, service playing, and organ literature. Prior to his appointment at Concordia, Blersch served as cantor of Trinity Lutheran Church, Peoria, IL; associate professor of music and music department chair at Concordia University, Ann Arbor, MI; and as an elementary music specialist in the Brunswick City Schools, Brunswick, OH.

Barry L. Bobb worked in various capacities at Concordia Publishing House; served various congregations in the St. Louis area as teacher and musician; currently serves as director of sanctuary music at Carmel Lutheran Church, Carmel, IN; and is the director of the Center for Church Music. His encouragement helped bring this project into fruition.

Steven Egler is professor of organ at Central Michigan University in Mount Pleasant, MI. Throughout his career, Egler has been a champion of new music and constantly has students studying the music of Charles Ore. An active church musician, Egler has served several churches in Illinois and Michigan for over 45 years, including his past post as director of music and organist of First Presbyterian Church in Mt. Pleasant, and his current position as artist in residence at First Congregational Church in Saginaw, MI.

David Held came to Concordia in Seward, NE, in 1979 where he directed the Concordia Singers. Prior to Concordia, Held served as teacher and director of music at Immanuel Lutheran Church, Waterloo, IA, and at St. John Lutheran Church, Orange, CA. In the early 1980s he served the Missouri Synod by introducing the hymnal *Lutheran Worship* around the United States. Since his retirement in 2000, he continues to serve as a supervisor of student teaching.

Kenneth T. Kosche is professor of music emeritus from Concordia University Wisconsin, where he served for 31 years, retiring in 2009. A parish musician at heart, his compositions include some 450 works in the catalogs of 16 American publishers, written for voices, instruments, organ, and handbells. In retirement he and his wife Rosemary live in Billings, MT, where he continues to play the organ, assist with the choir, and compose.

Connie Ore (1937–2010) received both her bachelor of science degree in education and her master's degree in family life science from Concordia University, Seward, NE. She taught elementary school in Chicago (1959–60) and Niles, IL (1960–61). She served as director of music at St. John Lutheran Church, Seward (1979–2001), where she was organist, choir director, and junior high music teacher. She wrote texts for several of her husband Charles' compositions.

Nancy Raabe is editor of *In Tempo,* a publication of the Association of Lutheran Church Musicians (ALCM). She serves at Atonement Lutheran Church in Beloit, WI. A classical music critic for many years, her books are published by Concordia Publishing House, MorningStar Music Publishers, and Lutheran University Press. Her music for worship is published by Augsburg Fortress, Choristers Guild, Hope Publishing Company, and others.

William A. Raabe, a professor of taxation and accountancy for 40 years, endowed the ALCM Raabe Prize for Excellence in Sacred Composition and is a member of the Founders Group for the Center for Church Music at Concordia University Chicago, both in conjunction with Nancy Raabe.

Steven P. Starke is pastor of St. John Lutheran Church in Amelith, MI. He is the author of over 175 hymns, including 32 in *Lutheran Service Book* (LSB), the most recent hymnal of The Lutheran Church—Missouri Synod. He served as chairman of the hymnody committee for the Lutheran Hymnal Project that led to the 2006 release of LSB. In 2011 Concordia Publishing House released *We Praise You and Acknowledge You, O Lord*, the first CD collection of Starke's hymns.

Financial Supporters

Dr. Ken Barjenbruch
Ivan and Irene Beethe
Nathan Beethe
Barry and Donna Bobb
Jim and Sharon Coe
Edward Dettling
Mr. and Mrs. Sam Eatherton
Dr. John Eggert
Larry Finke
George Frank
John Frank
Ren Frank
Mrs. Barbara Fremder
Karen Haak
Michael Held
Dr. Joseph Herl
John Horak
Matt Jansen
Jonathan Kohrs
Lincoln Chapter—AGO
Dr. James Marriott
Dr. Christelle Menth
Jonathan Mueller
Rev. Dr. and Mrs. William G. Moorhead
Brian Pfoltner
Dr. David Polley
Pam Steiner
John and Sara Young
Zion Lutheran Church/Wausau, WI